Bud's Easy™
Note Taking System

How To Take

Great Notes

In Class and

From Texts

Use Latest Brain Research

To Learn Super Study Skills

And Become An A+ Student

James Roberts

Lawrence House Publishers

Larchmont, New York

How to Take Great Notes in Class and From Texts

Fifth Edition

ISBN 978-1-891707-11-7

Trademarks
   Trademarked names appear in this book. The publisher states that it used trademarked names only for editorial purposes and to the benefit of the trademark owner with no intention of infringing on those trademarks.

   Every effort has been made to make this book as complete and accurate as possible, but no warranty or fitness is implied. The publisher assumes no responsibility for errors or omissions, or for damages resulting from the use of the information contained herein.

Published by Lawrence House Publishers
Larchmont, New York 10538

Contents

Chapter 3
How To Powerize Your Memory

PART II

Chapter 4
Take Great Notes In Class

Chapter 5
Take Great Notes From Texts

Introduction

There is no easy way to become a successful A+ student. While it is true that school work comes easier to some, the rest of us can also hit the mark. But it takes real effort and drive.

How can you possibly remember all the information that your teachers give you in lectures and that you read in texts? No doubt a daunting task! In recent years research in brain function using functional magnetic resonance imaging has helped us to understand better exactly how humans learn and how our memories work.

For example, scientists have identified at least six different long term memory areas where we file information. If you know how to use these memory banks, you will be better able to recall the data that we are expected to learn.

This book explains how you can use note taking as a tool to improve your ability to learn and remember the volumes of information you get in lectures and texts. You will learn the basic skills of good note taking. They are broken down into specific, easy to remember components. With a little practice you will be on the path to becoming an A+ student.

The system does require some preparation of your note books in special formats for lecture notes and text notes. However, note book preparation is simple and accomplished in a few minutes.

The rest is up to you. Like the accomplished musician, low handicap golfer, or top notch athlete, you must decide that you will practice, practice, and practice until the skills of note taking and studying from notes become automatic.

Good luck with your goal of becoming an A+ student!

Chapter 1

THE SKILL OF NOTE TAKING

WHAT IS A SKILL?

A skill is defined in the American Heritage Dictionary as follows:

1. *Proficiency, facility, or dexterity that is acquired or developed through training or experience.*
2. *An art, trade or technique particularly one requiring the use of hands or body.*
3. *A developed talent or ability: writing skills.*

All through your life you have been developing skills. Just think of all those you have acquired. As a five year old you learned to tie your shoelaces. That was a tough one. Later, you learned to balance your two wheeler without training wheels. Gradually you acquired the myriad skills that make it possible for you to function as an adult. Any task you do that requires you to use your hands or body is a skill.

Think of learning to play the piano. How difficult! The beginner must learn to read music and associate the printed notes with the keyboard. The fingers are placed on the keys. Slowly, the brain learns to send messages to the fingers to strike certain keys. Only through regular, spaced practice can anyone become a top pianist. It is amazing that once the skill becomes embedded, the muscles seem to develop a memory of their own and they easily respond to the brain's messages.

Learning a sports skill is no different. Good tennis players and golfers practice many hours, honing the strokes, creating images in the brain that send messages to muscles that memorize the motions that generate the great tennis serve or the perfect chip, drive, or putt in golf.

Low level skills such as brushing your teeth, tying your shoe laces, or cutting your steak are easily learned. We are barely aware that they are skills. The tough ones: learning to ski, learning to play a musical instrument, or learning to take notes in class or from a text require sustained effort and practice. Motivation is important. If you have a strong desire to master a skill, the time needed is reduced. Example: How long did it take you to learn to send text messages at high speed?

HOW DO WE LEARN NEW SKILLS?

1.   We break down the skill into its several components.   For example, when learning to word process on a QWERTY desktop or laptop keyboard you would identify the components like this:

First component: Learn the "home keys" on which your fingers sit at rest: ASDF for the left hand and JKL; for the right hand.

Second component: Learn the finger muscle motion needed to press the home keys to get a letter on the computer screen.

2. Practice. Here's an old joke: A tourist asks someone in New York, "How do I get to Carnegie Hall?" The New Yorker answers, "Practice, practice, practice!

To master any skill practice is a must. In word processing you must practice the movement needed to type the letters "J" and "F." with the pointer finger of each hand. You must train your finger muscles to strike the keys automatically without thinking or looking down at the keys by building muscle memory. And so you begin, almost child-like, to type FFF - JJJ with the index fingers of your left and right hands respectively. You check to make sure that your hands are at the correct angle and that the proper pressure and rhythm are used. You watch the computer screen to be sure you are hitting the correct keys.

Educational psychologists have learned that frequent, short periods of practice are much more powerful than single, long periods. It is better to practice in three separate ten minute drill sessions spaced during the day than in one thirty minute session. In the long session, fatigue, loss of attention, and distractions detract from the value of the practice. You must be committed to spending sufficient time for practice to develop mastery of any high level skill.

Where are we going with all this discussion about skills?

Believe it or not, note taking is a skill just like playing the piano because it fits the definition of an activity that requires you to use your body and your mind together to allow you to do something automatically and without very much conscious thought. Note taking is a skill that must be broken down into its component parts and practiced frequently. You have been taught many "school" skills, but unfortunately few schools take the time to teach note taking. It is an important skill that is absolutely necessary for success in school.

A bit later in this book you will learn how to break note taking down into its component parts and learn how to practice each one. Since it is a relatively high level skill, not unlike piano playing or keyboarding, it will require practice and commitment. Remember, one does not become a fine pianist, tennis player, or skier without motivation and desire. You will need a healthy supply of these last traits to succeed.

NOTE TAKING AND SCHOOL GRADES

Researchers have discovered that effective note taking has a high correlation with outstanding school achievement. Many studies have shown the positive effect of good note taking on achievement. Even more significant is the effectiveness of students' reviewing and studying their notes to prepare for tests. Note taking should be a major weapon in your arsenal of learning tools.

Note Taking is an Important Skill Because It:

■ Forces you to be an active listener and reader
■ Enables you to digest and understand information
■ Helps you summarize lectures and texts
■ Helps you organize data
■ Helps you study for tests
■ Improves your memory
■ Helps raise your grades

NOTE TAKING AND LEARNING

So note taking is an important skill and it is going to improve your grades, help you study for tests, and improve your memory. How will note taking accomplish all this? It will do it because note taking is a skill that facilitates learning. We learn because our brains can remember. We could not learn to play the piano if after diligent practice sessions we could not remember the notes or remember how to move our fingers. What a waste that would be! All that practice gone! Note taking facilitates learning by helping our brains to remember information.

Note taking helps students to focus while learning and helps them think through and absorb information more fully. Moreover, as new material is presented in subsequent lectures or readings, note taking helps students link the new information with that previously learned.

HOW DO I KNOW I CAN DO IT?

In case you're thinking that improving study and note taking skills are too tough for you, consider these ideas:

■ Success in school and life is more a matter of will and drive than innate ability. Remember Edison's oft quoted comment, "Genius is ten percent inspiration and ninety percent perspiration."

■ Most people use only a tiny part of their potential. Imagine what you can accomplish if you really get going.

■ We tend to be held back by our own feelings of doubt and some outmoded beliefs. Most of us have enough basic intelligence and ability to handle any of today's jobs or professions if we are determined to succeed.

■ Consider the popular marathon races. The first to come across the finish line and the last have all come the same distance. So it is with school. If you master all the material in a course, you will know just as much as the fastest student in the class. It may simply take you a little longer, but your "A" will be worth just as much.

■ Think of yourself as a winner and you will be one!

■ Winners, people who succeed, set goals for themselves. The most successful set a long range goal and then lay out a series of short term goals designed to carry them along the road to achieving their main objective.

A WORD TO THOSE WHO HAVE TROUBLE LEARNING

Suppose you find school challenging. You don't always catch on to what your teachers are trying to explain. You read assignments, but half way through a page you find it hard to remember what you've read. Your confidence is shaken. You think maybe you don't have a high enough IQ?

Psychologists now know there is really no such thing as a single IQ number that determines how you do in school and life. As a matter of fact, we know that people learn in different ways and have different kinds of intelligence. Some have great language skills, some have better mathematical intelligence, some have a kind of practical intelligence or street smarts that helps them respond quickly to problems, some are gifted musically, while others excel at personal relationships.

There are legions of people who reportedly had difficult times in school who later achieved remarkable success in careers in every field.

Here are just a few:

Tom Cruise, actor	Whoopi Goldberg, actress
Magic Johnson, athlete	Thomas Edison, inventor
Harrison Ford, actor	John Lennon, musician
Jay Leno, comedian	Robin Williams, actor
Albert Einstein, scientist	Nolan Ryan, athlete
Danny Glover, actor	Andy Warhol, artist
Anderson Cooper, journalist	Winston Churchill, statesman

But these folks decided they wanted to overcome shortcomings and determined to succeed. Even if you have had trouble learning, this book will show you how to be an active learner and become an A+ student. Set your goal to be a successful learner through note taking and you will achieve greatness!

Be a Winner!

Set Your Personal Goals

Here is your Long Term Goal:

I will be successful in school by becoming an active learner through effective note taking in class and from texts!

Here are your Short Term goals:

I will train to learn Bud's Easy Note Taking System for the next two weeks.

I will master the skill sets for great note taking described in this book.

After two weeks I will be able to use Bud's Easy Note Taking System in class and from texts.

I will continue to practice the skill sets to increase my speed and accuracy through out the semester.

I will become more confident in class and see improvement in class participation and test grades.

In the next chapter we will explore what learning theorists have begun to discover about how our brains work and how we remember and actually learn.

Chapter 2
Understanding Memory Research

We go to school to learn. But how does "learning" actually occur?. What happens in our brains when we read a textbook, listen to a lecture, or watch an educational film? How do we sort out the important ideas from the unimportant? How do we remember significant material? Why do some people seem to learn more easily than others?

This chapter will explain how we respond to the words and sounds we read or hear and the images we see and how we use them in our attempts to learn new information. By understanding the way your brain processes new data, you will know how to use your brain to help you learn and remember. Let's get started with a basic picture of how our brains work.

Latest Memory Research

Beginning with the ancient Egyptians, on to Plato, Aristotle, and Socrates, and continuing through the centuries humans have puzzled and theorized about the human mind and how it works. The mysteries of how the brain controls our emotions, activities, and learning have been explored endlessly. Recent advances in technology have opened exciting new research possiblities.

A new research area known as cognitive neuroscience attempts to understand what happens in the brain and nervous system when we perceive, comprehend, and learn.

Physicians regularly use magnetic resonance imaging (MRI) to identify tumors and other medical problems. Now psychologists use a technique known as fMRI or functional magnetic resonance imaging to observe changes in the brains of living subjects. While subjects receive various stimuli or carry out different tasks, fMRI provides thousands of images of the brain. Researchers have observed that specific areas of the brain "light up" with bright colors when subjects are reading, watching a scary movie, or solving a difficult mathematics problem.

We are a long way from fully grasping how humans learn and remember. However, the fMRI studies and other research has led to a growing consensus around the concepts of sensory memory, short term/working memory, and long term memory. Researchers are beginning to understand how these memory traces affect our learning. In the following pages we will explain how scientists now believe we learn through memory.

Sensory Memory

Sensory memory is where we *consciously* process new stimuli that we receive through our five senses: hearing, seeing, tasting, smelling, and touching. We are totally aware of the stimuli. We know that we are experiencing sounds, images, tastes, odors, and skin sensations and we are fully cognizant of our attempts to deal with them.

Sound stimuli can only be held for seconds in sensory memory before they disappear. An example of a sound stimuli would be a telephone number a friend gives you. Most people can only hold a new phone number in sensory memory until they finish dialing.

Visual stimuli are also retained only for a brief lapse of time. Suppose a photograph were flashed on a screen for five seconds and then removed. If you were asked to describe the photograph, you would have great difficulty remembering more than a few details.

Some researchers believe that the reason sensory memories are so brief is to protect our short term and long term memories from overloading with unimportant data.

Short Term Memory

When you receive a visual or sound stimulus in sensory memory it is instantly directed to short term memory where it again lasts only seconds. Short term memory is where we store sensory stimuli if we only need to quickly repeat the information.

Our ability to hold data in short term memory is affected by distractions. If you are trying to remember a phone number someone just orally gave you and you had to answer your phone before you could write it down, you might not be able to recall the number.

Working Memory

Working memory goes one step further. It takes data from short term memory and holds it briefly so it can be used later for other actions such as problem solving, reasoning, and learning. For example, when someone gives you a phone number and you know that you will have to dial the number shortly, you shift the number into working memory and try to do something to hold the number longer until you can write it down. Most people resort to repeating the number silently or out loud over and over.

Psychologists can measure people's short term and working memory using tests that ask subjects to repeat a series of numbers or to recall a series of visual symbols. People who can remember more numbers in a series or more symbols can be said to have better short term and working memory. For example, air traffic controllers need excellent working memory because they must listen for the call signs as aircraft call in, hold the call signs in working memory, then issue flight instructions. Controllers often work several aircraft within seconds. Similarly, pilots must listen for their call signs, hear their instructions, repeat them to the controller who verifies accuracy, and hold the instructions in working memory until they can comply.

Working memory is extremely important in problem solving. For example, if you had to solve this problem without writing it down,

$$X = 218 - 9 + 7$$

most likely you would subtract 9 from 218 to get 209. You would then keep the 209 in working memory while you try to recall the next step, adding 7, to get the answer 216. You had to remember the question, the result of the first computation, and the last task to get the final answer. You use the same basic process when answering verbal test questions or when reading a book.

However, there are limits to working memory. If you asked for driving directions and someone said:

"Go one block to the traffic light, turn right, go two blocks, and you will see the church on your left."

you would probably have no difficulty holding the directions in your working memory until you reached the church.

On the other hand if you heard:

"Go one block to the traffic light, turn right and go two blocks till you see the church on your left, turn right at the church, go two miles past three traffic lights and turn left on Highway 98, go a half mile and look for the billboard on your left and turn into the restaurant parking lot."

no doubt you would have trouble holding all that data in your working memory and you would probably have to stop again for directions.

The more information you can hold in working memory, the better you will be at problem solving. As a matter of fact, working memory may be a good predictor of semantic intelligence.

When we receive stimuli in working memory we hold them a few seconds just long enough to connect with long term memories stored away. As we concentrate on the stimulus received, we activate related long term memories that allow us to solve problems or to take necessary action. We need working memory to carry out many of the ordinary tasks of daily living such as cooking, dressing, or talking with friends. When a teacher describes a scientific event such as a lunar eclipse, we will almost instantaneously begin recalling data in long term memory about the sun, the moon, rotation, revolution, light and many other bits of information we have previously stored in long term memory about the solar system and the earth.

Short term and working memory can be sustained a bit longer than sensory memory, lasting up to 20 seconds. George Miller, a Harvard psychologist, found that humans can only recall 7 items plus or minus 2 in working memory. He called it the Magic 7. Isn't it interesting that phone numbers contain seven digits!

By consciously processing the stimuli you are able to retain visual and auditory stimuli in working memory for longer periods. Combining bits of data or "chunking" can make remembering easier. For example, suppose you were asked to recall a series of 19 letters such as: FLUSAINNASAUNNBACIA. You would probably have difficulty even if you tried to repeat all the letters several times. However, if you "chunked" the 19 letters into 7 chunks like this: FL - USA - IN - NASA - UN - NBA - CIA you would have much less difficulty.

Long Term Memory

Six Long Term Memory Areas

We can store and access a tremendous amount of information in long term memory. It is like the hard drive in your computer with the difference that your long term memory brain "drive" has an enormous, perhaps unlimited capacity. We are constantly moving data from our working memory to our long term memory area.

Some data become permanently stored in long term memory without any conscious help from us. For example, most people cannot get the picture of the World Trade Center buildings collapsing out of their minds. Other information that we would love to make permanent such as some mathematical equations, chemical formulas, or historical events just don't seem to stick for most of us.

Your goal in reading this book is to learn how to make information in your long term memory as permanent as you can. You want to be able to recall it for tests or to use it to carry out functions. This chapter and the next will give you important suggestions for improving your long term memory!

Brain researchers now believe there are at least six long term memory areas: Procedural, Semantic, Emotional, Episodic, Automatic Response, and Spatial. Data we receive in working memory may move to one or more of these long term storage areas.

Procedural Memory

Any physical action that uses a combination of mental activity (reading sheet music and sending messages through the nerves to the fingers) and physical activity (striking piano keys) that we can do without thinking comes from the procedural memory part of long term memory.

Driving a car, playing tennis, and playing a guitar are examples of procedures in which muscles spontaneously respond to mental stimuli. Procedural memory is where all of our learned skills are stored. You have already mastered thousands of such procedures. Your goal is to get the skill of note taking embedded in your procedural memory!

The beginning guitar player must think very consciously about what she is doing. The learner must look at the music, visually check the location of the strings, carefully place the fingers, and then probably look up at the music again before actually strumming the guitar. This is the way you slowly and painstakingly begin to learn new procedures or skills. Only after considerable and regular practice can the seasoned acoustic guitarist play well without conscious thought. The more the guitarist practices, the more automatic her skill becomes, and the more beautiful the music!

Procedural Memory and Note Taking

Because note taking will be the foundation for building your long term memory of texts and lectures, you should understand the similarity of note taking to guitar playing or bike riding. Procedural memories become increasingly more deeply embedded as you practice. Think of how much more confidence you have as a bike rider now compared with how you felt during your first attempts to balance without training wheels. You can now ride with one hand and talk at the same time!

Your ability to take notes spontaneously without conscious thought will improve rapidly with practice. You have many opportunities to practice every time you are in a class listening to a lecture or reading a text so your skills should improve very quickly. Before long you will be taking notes and studying almost without thinking. You will gradually take notes more fully, more quickly, and more efficiently! Chapter 3 will provide detailed instructions for building the procedural memory of note taking!

Before you begin learning to build your long term procedural memory of note taking, let's explore the latest research in the other five long term memory areas.

Semantic Memory

Known also as declarative or explicit memory, semantic memory is the big kahuna of them all because semantic information is language information. Our semantic memory is filled with things we "know" intuitively. For example, we "know" that paint comes in many colors. We "know" that fish are vertebrates. We know that water freezes at zero degrees centigrade. Virtually everything we describe as "knowledge" resides in semantic memory.

Words and images are the source of our "knowing." In school situations we are constantly listening to lectures in class and reading from texts to enlarge our knowledge base. Gradually, our semantic memory grows as we come to "know" more and more. Unfortunately, much of the knowledge we receive will gradually fade from our long term memory unless we take specific steps to embed it deeply.

Your challenge as a student is to be able to recall at will the specific knowledge that you need at a particular moment from the immense hard drive of your long term memory. You need to recall dates, formulas, concepts, and ideas to take action demanded by a new stimulus received in working memory. Frequently, the immediate stimulus is a question on a quarterly examination in one of your school classes. Your working memory is stimulated by the reading of the test question. Immediately synapses form to reach into your long term memory for the knowledge needed to answer the question in working memory. The most frequently tested and graded stuff is data you hope is stored in your long term semantic memory.

When working memory stimuli (the question on the exam) call for the information in long term memory, you will not be able to recall it if the data has not been laid down in strong, clear, powerful terms. Information received in long term semantic memory must be kneaded, squeezed, stretched and frequently reinforced to make sure it sticks. In the next chapter we will explore some techniques for processing data in long term memory so it can be easily recalled. But first, let's look at the other long term memory storage areas. Some of them can help reinforce data in our semantic memory.

Emotional Memory

During an emotional experience we lay down very strong, clear traces in our long term emotional memory. David Goleman, a researcher, believes that this is the most powerful of all the memory areas. Some images, like the World Trade Center attack or the funeral of a loved one, are transferred almost immediately to your long term emotional memory bank. Data accompanied by fear, sadness, joy, anger, or other strong emotions tend to be firmly and permanently implanted in this powerful, long term memory area.

A particularly emotional event such as an accident or hospital stay will probably reinforce your semantic memory. For example, you may have lots of medical information already stored in long term memory. You understand fever, infection, antibiotics, allergies, and loads of other data. However, if you are injured in an accident, the emotional memories of your treatment will strongly reinforce many of your stored semantic memories.

Unfortunately, a strong emotion like fear can sometimes trigger the "flight or fight" response. The adrenalin rush that prepares the body can short circuit access to other memory areas. Panic deprives us of the ability to think clearly and to call up important information stored in long term memory. Even those trained to deal with emergency situations sometimes find that they cannot recall the proper actions to take to save their own lives.

Emotions can similarly wreak havoc in test situations. Have you ever opened a test booklet, glanced at the questions, felt overwhelmed by the scope of the test, and found that your mind had gone blank. Information firmly stored in long term memory was suddenly inaccessible.

Episodic Memory

When we remember events, the times and places they occurred, and anything we learned during the event we are plumbing our episodic memory. Once you have experienced an event or episode, it is stored and the data surrounding the event can be easily recalled. Your recollection of the World Trade Center attack is an example of a deeply and strongly embedded episodic memory reinforced by the co-existing emotional memory of the event.

Episodic memories can change and embellish semantic memories. For example, our semantic memory is full of data about skyscrapers and airplanes, but the episodic memory of the World Trade Center attack will modify our knowledge base.

Episodes that are highly emotional such as an accident, an illness, or a death in the family will likely be more easily and vividly remembered than events that are more benign. However, such memories may affect the accuracy of our semantic memory.

Automatic Response Memory

The researcher, E. Jensen, found that we learn many automatic responses as we grow and learn. When we gain approval or satisfaction following a stimulus, we gradually build an automatic response to the stimulus. There is a huge quantity of data in your automatic response long term memory. All the addition, subtraction, multiplication, and division facts (2+6=8, 4-6=2, 2x9=18, etc.) that you learned in elementary school using flash cards and drills are there. You hear the first few bars of a melody and immediately the entire song pours out. Automatic response memory and procedural memory are somewhat inter-related. Much of what we use in procedural memory may be partly an automatic response as when we respond to musical cues.

Spatial Memory

Spatial memory is what we develop as we form images of our location in space. For example, if you had to enter your bedroom at night during a blackout, you could probably navigate fairly well without bumping into furniture. You have in your spatial memory bank the location and distances of the furniture in the room.

Spatial memory also allows us to follow directions. If you arrived at an airport in a strange city, your spatial memory would enable you to reach a destination by responding to specific directions: "Go to the first traffic light, turn left, go three miles until you reach a MacDonalds on your right, turn left at that intersection, go a half mile and you will see the entrance to the campus on your right." Spatial memory gives us a sense of where we are in space. We "know" left from right, we can judge distances, and recognize landmarks.

Summary

Now that you understand how your memory works, it is easy to see that if you remember something you have learned it. If you remember how to tie your shoes, you have learned how to tie your shoes. If you remember how to solve an equation, you have learned how to solve an equation. If you remember how to play a scale, you have learned how to play a scale.

So what is important in learning is strengthening memory. In the next chapter you will learn how to do just that. And the primary tool for improving and strengthening your memory will be note taking!

Here is the most important equation in education:

Remembering = Learning

Chapter 3

HOW TO POWERIZE YOUR MEMORY

You now have a basic understanding of how information flows from an exposure to a stimulus into sensory memory, then into short term or working memory, and finally into one or more of your long term memory areas. Your goal is to improve your memory and be able to retrieve important information when needed.

Let's review what you've learned about how information moves into your brain and memory. When you sit in class listening to your teacher talk, you get sound stimuli from her voice. When she writes words or diagrams on the black board, you receive visual stimuli.

The sounds and images last seconds in sensory memory before they move to short term and working memory. You hold the stimuli in working memory ready to use them to solve problems, initiate an action, or connect with other data stored in long term memory. In seconds you begin moving the new information into long term memory where you want to store it for future retrieval. You want to get the new information to "stick" in your long term memory so it will be available when you need it!

In this chapter we will give you practical suggestions for powerizing your long term memory so you can reach your goal.

LIFESTYLE AFFECTS MEMORY
DIET

Diet affects memory and learning. Unfortunately, most Americans eat diets of processed foods loaded with fat, sugar and refined grains. We have high rates of Type 2 diabetes, cancer, cardiovascular disease and obesity. The brain and your memory depend on an abundant blood supply. Eating the "American" diet of fast food, donuts, cakes, fries, wings, and stuff from cans, wreaks havoc with the arteries.

Diets high in saturated fats and bad carbs have a deleterious effect causing artery clogging and reduction in the flow of blood to the brain. Too many students eat processed foods loaded with high fructose corn syrup. The sugar in a bottled soda may give you a temporary high, but it is followed by feelings of fatigue. Sodas also add calories and pounds!

Good foods that contain anti-oxidants protect against free radicals that damage brain cells. Eating lots of fruits and vegetables, especially highly colored foods like blueberries, red grapes, and green vegetables is good for your brain. Fish, lean meats, low or non-fat dairy products also protect your brain health.

Your brain depends on a good supply of glucose carried by your blood. That's why it is always good to eat something like a piece of fruit or whole grain cereal before you sit for an exam or a study session. If you want to powerize your memory, pay attention to what you eat!

SLEEP

Sleep is an important component of good health. Plan your life so you can complete all the varied tasks of daily life in an orderly manner including getting 6-8 hours of uninterrupted sleep. You will avoid the stress that comes from feeling tired. There is even some evidence that memories are reinforced during the resting stages of sleep when we are not bombarded with new stimuli.

Many students believe that pulling "all nighters" cramming for exams is the best strategy for test preparation. Not really! When you walk into the exam room you will be tired and probably have trouble staying on task. Moreover, cramming rams data into your short term memory where it will fade after a few days. You may get a passing grade on the quiz you crammed for, but by the time you get to the final exam, most of what you crammed will be gone.

EXERCISE

Numerous studies show that voluntary exercise enhances learning and memory. Exercise increases blood flow that helps the brain function. Regular exercise like jogging, playing tennis, or participating in team sports makes us feel healthier and reduces stress. Budget some time every day to break a sweat!

POSITIVE ATTITUDE

We remember best those concepts that are meaningful and interesting to us. Think of how much you know about your favorite hobby. Baseball fans know the names, batting averages, and all the statistics of their favorite players and a host of others as well. Jazz afficionados know the music and stories of all the greats. If you have a driving interest, remarkably, you can store loads of information in your long term memory without even trying! Why? A positive attitude stimulates brain cell function.

What does this tell you about your attitude toward school? If you sit through classes bored and inattentive your chances of moving learning to long term memory are nil.

That's why it is critical to develop a positive attitude toward school. Think of the new and exciting information you will learn. Change negative thoughts about courses to positive thoughts. What good will reading Hamlet be for you? If you're thinking it's a waste of time, you are going to have a tough time learning anything about Shakespeare.

Think of how fortunate you are to be in a school where knowledge doors are constantly opening. Try to relate what you are learning in class to your own life experience. Think of the rewards that will accrue if you succeed.

Use all the resources available to help you increase your motivation. Your school may even have a study or homework help center. Find and make friends with people who are successful and motivated. Talk to them about their goals and the techniques they use to learn. Join a study group.

ORGANIZATION

Face it. You probably have a lot to do. Maybe you have to work part time. Perhaps you have family obligations. These things take time, but if you get organized you can handle everything.

Keep a log for a couple of days of all your activities noting the times you began and ended each activity including sleep. You may find out that you are using big chunks of time doing unimportant things that eat into your productive hours. How much time do you watch TV? Are you endlessly text messaging, Twittering and Facebooking for hours? Examine your log to identify time wasters.

Build a daily and weekly calendar that will allot appropriate blocks of time for each activity. Block out sufficient study time for each course. Study periods are for homework and review. Study time must have a high priority over non-essential activities. Your stress level will be reduced when you find that you have time for everything in your busy schedule.

You must give high priority to classroom time and study time and be sure you are actively engaged - not just sitting through the sessions. Decide that you will never miss a class or study session!

LEARNING STYLES

We are all hard-wired to learn in different ways. Some folks learn best by listening, others by seeing, and others by manipulating or touching objects. There are many different descriptions of learning styles, but all are based on three basic styles: visual, auditory, and kinesthetic.

Do you know how you learn best? If you know, you can use your most powerful learning style to advantage to build strong memory traces in your long term memory areas.

Study the descriptions of learning styles below to see what type of learner you are. You will probably find that you tend to enjoy learning in one or more of the styles.

Visual Verbal Learner

You like to see information written on blackboards, in PowerPoint, or other projected images.
You like to have an written outline before a lecture.
You learn best from reading a textbook.
You like taking notes for review.
You can recall news stories better when you read them in a newspaper or see them on TV than when you hear them on the radio.
You find it difficult to follow lecturers who do not write blackboard notes.

Auditory Verbal Learner

You like to listen to your teachers deliver lectures.
You enjoy class discussions and remember the main points.
You can remember lectures you hear on audio tapes.

You can remember the voice and tone of a teacher making important points.

You can remember information if you recite it out loud.

You enjoy speaking out in class and giving oral reports.

You are good at remembering names.

You can follow oral directions easily.

You do well with study groups.

Visual-Nonverbal Learner

You find it easier to remember information presented with photographs or diagrams.

You like teachers who show films and use charts and diagrams extensively.

You spend time studying pictures, graphs, and diagrams in texts, newspapers, and magazines and retain the information.

You remember things more easily when you can picture them in your mind's eye.

You enjoy photography, design, and art forms.

Tactile Kinesthetic Learner

You enjoy "hands on" activities when you can manipulate materials.

You like laboratory classes best.

You like to be able to move about a classroom rather than remain seated for long periods.

You enjoy field trips where you can touch materials.

You like role playing.

You may not have great handwriting or spelling skills.

You tend to be handy.

Were you able to identify your learning style or styles? If you did, you now know something about the learning situations in which you are most comfortable. Keep in mind that these descriptions are general and you may find you use parts of all three styles. Later, we will identify specific ways you can use your learning style strengths.

You are now ready to learn how to powerize all of your memory areas. You know that diet, sleep, exercise and a positive attitude are important. You know you must commit to real time on task to get the rewards of study. Now let's find out how to powerize your procedural memory which is the basis of note taking.

BUILDING PROCEDURAL MEMORY
The Basis of Note Taking

This book is about using note taking to improve your memory and enhance your learning. Your goal is to make note taking an automatic, unconscious skill like driving or playing an instrument. Now here is the bad news. Regular, intensive practice is required to excel in any skill. There is no other way.

Deliberate Practice

Researchers have found that many of the world's top athletes, musicians, and business executives did not start with any special gift. A combination of high achievement motivation and "deliberate practice" make the great musicians, athletes and stars.

Great golfers spend hours each week practicing and perfecting each challenging stroke in golf. Golf pros hit hundreds of balls every day. Concert musicians spend hours each day practicing and playing in an effort to perfect their performances. The great athletes and musicians of the world have the motivation and drive to be the best. But they can only achieve the heights by constant "deliberate practice."

"Deliberate practice" is a special procedure that outstanding performers in all fields use to master their skills. They select a skill component, set a goal, attempt the skill, evaluate the result, adjust their technique and try again to improve. The practice is repeated hundreds of times until the performer is satisfied with the result.

Many golfers go to the range once a week and hit a bucket of balls, but never get any better. Champion golfers practice by hitting a 9 iron 200 times from 150 yards with the goal of getting the ball to land within 20 feet of the flag 90% percent of the time. They observe each shot, adjust after each one, and constantly try to improve as they practice for several hours. Musicians do the same practicing parts of compositions until they are satisfied.

Because note taking is a skill that is built on procedural memory, you must use "deliberate practice" to master it. This means you must break down the components of note taking just as the golfer identifies the parts of his 9 iron swing or a tennis player scrutinizes the parts of her serve.

In Chapter 4 you will learn the specific skill sets of note taking and begin to practice them. But if you really want to be a big league student, you must commit to regular "deliberate practice." You must set a goal to improve each component of note taking, try it, see how well you have done, repeat and try to improve. Each time you must strive to perform better on that skill set than you did on the last trial.

If you are motivated to become an A+ student, you will do what it takes and do it with enthusiasm. All it takes is PRACTICE, PRACTICE, PRACTICE!

BUILDING SEMANTIC MEMORY

Long term semantic memory can be enhanced using the techniques that follow:

■ Add new data to an "advance organizer" or organizational framework that already exists in your memory.

An "advance organizer" is information you acquire about the subject prior to learning something new. You use advance organizers to get a preview of new learning. Assume you are planning to watch a TV program on immigration reform. First, you do a Google search and get a quick overview of the subject. Then when you watch the program, you will see how the new information "fits" into the data you learned from the Google search. With the advantage of the advance organizer, you find it easier to assimilate the new information and store it in long term memory.

A teacher's printed outline or handout before a lecture is an advance organizer that will give you a framework on which to attach new facts you will learn during the lecture. Visual learners love these outlines and handouts.

We have our own internal advance organizers in the form of memories of each of the subjects we have learned over the years. We have studied history, science, literature, mathematics, and many other subjects and have a memory store of each embedded in our semantic memories. We study American history several times during a school career. Each repetition adds new information to the existing framework built by the earlier learnings.

During a class lesson on Reconstruction, we recall, almost sub-consciously, what we previously learned in school of the Civil War and its aftermath . Each time we receive new information it finds its place on the already existing framework and it "sticks." As you do advanced study try to recall the older learnings and see where the new knowledge fits on the existing framework you have already stored. Your prior knowledge is a basic kind of advance organizer.

Before reading a new text chapter prepare an advance organizer. Look through the table of contents to get an overview of the chapter. Scan the chapter for bold face paragraph headings and recite them out loud. Can you see how they relate to each other? Recite all the headings from memory. Make a written outline using the major headings and sub-headings of the chapter. Try to see the whole picture of a chapter before you read it. Later, as you read intensively, you will know the general framework of the whole chapter and understand how each section fits into the whole scheme. You will be attaching new information to the framework of your outline advance organizer. Advance organizers are important foundations for building semantic memory. Although this is a technique that visual learners like to use, it is important for aural and kinesthetic learners to employ it as well. Visual learners do well by seeing the chapter in their mind's eye while aural learners improve semantic memory by reciting.

Learning a theory, law, or principle before reading or hearing about examples or supporting ideas also serves as an advance organizer. Because you know the law or theory, you will better understand how the example or supporting idea relates to the theory and how it fits on the framework of the theory. For example, in economics the law of diminishing returns states that at some point each additional unit of input yields less and less output. If you learned that law first, it would be easy for you to understand what was happening if a small chain of three retail clothing shops in a small city added a fourth and found that the chain's total sales dropped.

■ Review recently learned material just before hearing or reading new related information.

Reviewing, another form of advance organizer, ties the new data to the existing data. Reviewing helps lay down a strong, clear trace of the new data in semantic memory by joining it to earlier learnings.

Suppose you were studying the rise of democracy in a developing country. During a lecture on Monday you learn of two events:

1. The rise of an intellectual movement.
2. The growth of an entrepreneurial class.

Just before Wednesday's lecture you review your notes of the two events. During Wednesday's lecture you are ready to link what you are going to learn about a third event:

3. The fall of a military junta.

By tying the learnings of the Monday and Wednesday lectures together, you build a strong memory trace of the overall three event trend.

■ Identify the main ideas of all new data.

Identify the major concepts. Be aware that of the many words you hear or see when receiving new information only a few represent main ideas. The rest are subordinate ideas, examples, illustrations, or comparisons. Try to learn the difference. You must separate the main ideas from the rest and imprint a few strong, clear images of those ideas in your semantic memory. For example, as you jot down data, ask yourself: Is this the main idea? Is this only a supporting part of the main idea? Is this only an example? Is this only an illustration? Is this only a comparison?

You can get help identifying main ideas in texts and lectures. Bold headings in texts and underlined words or colored markers on white boards in class signify main ideas. Visual learners will grab these visual stimuli. Teachers may even call attention to important ideas by statements or just by a change in voice. If you hear, "This is one of the most important concepts to remember," you've heard a main idea. Aural learners will benefit when they cue on such oral remarks in lectures.

As you take notes underline or highlight the main ideas but not the supporting ideas, illustrations, or examples. Think about how the examples, illustrations, and comparisons relate to the main ideas.

The brain cannot remember all the details of an hour long lecture, but it can hold the main concepts if you consciously reduce what you have heard to only the most important ideas and lay down strong, powerful, clear memory traces. If you do not break the new data down into its main ideas, the brain receives a large blur of information that will be virtually impossible to recall.

■ Analyze information you want to store.

Analyzing and thinking about information helps to develop deeper memory traces. As you turn ideas over in your mind, you develop personal ownership of them. Asking yourself questions about new data is a method of analysis. How is this subject related to what you learned yesterday? How does the new information compare with other ideas you have? How does it contrast? The more you analyze, the easier it will be for you to recall the information.

■ Reduce ideas to symbols, maps, diagrams, and pictures.

Transform newly analyzed data into symbolic language. This requires higher order thinking and gives you ownership of the data by transforming the original concept into a symbol of your own making. For example, if you were taking notes on the westward expansion of the United States, you might draw a little sombrero to represent Mexican trade next to the notes you wrote. A crown for a king or an ax to portray an ancient battle will do.

Illustration 3.1. Example of data transformed into a symbol

You don't have to be an artist. Anything you draw that looks at all like the symbol will be fine. Symbols are easy to remember and will help you to recall the full information later. Visual learners like to use this technique, but all learners will profit if they use it. See Illustration 3.1 above.

Word "maps" make it easy to remember concepts. When trying to learn a complicated concept, analyze the main ideas and supporting ideas and arrange them in a "map." Think of how the ideas relate to each other. Enclose each word or phrase in a circle or oval. Join the main topics and supporting words or phrases with lines to show the relationships among them. See Illustration 3.2 below.

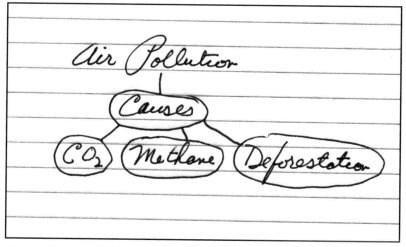

Illustration 3.2. Example of a word "map" showing relationships among ideas

Draw diagrams, graphs, and charts. You can more easily store a diagram in your long term memory than a written description of the same data. Analyze the data and design a diagram, chart, or graph that best illustrates the concept. Planning the diagram or chart forces you to visualize the data. Visual learners will love this technique, but everyone should use it to place a strong, positive concept in your semantic memory. See Illustration 3.3 below.

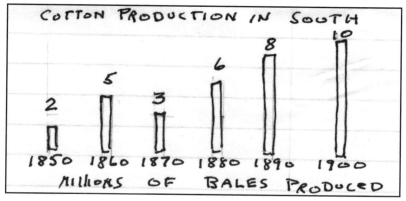

Illustration 3.3. Example of a graph describing data

■ Arrange ideas in groups or "chunks"

Group ideas together when presented with a great deal of information. Remember the rule of seven. You normally can hold seven plus or minus two bits of information in short term or working memory for just a few seconds. If you are presented with lots of data, arrange them in easily recognizable "chunks" that will help you move data to semantic memory.

For example, if you are studying the Middle East you will read and hear much about the various countries.

Suppose you are having trouble remembering the major countries of the Middle East. There are eight - one more than the magic seven: Saudi Arabia, Iran, Iraq, Jordan, Israel, Egypt, Turkey, and Syria. If you chunk them into two groups of three and five like this you will remember them easily. [Israel, Iran, Iraq] - [Jordan, Egypt, Syria, Saudia Arabia, Lebanon] to form the acronym: I I I - J E S S L.

You can do the same with any other difficult to remember data. See Illustration 3.4 below.

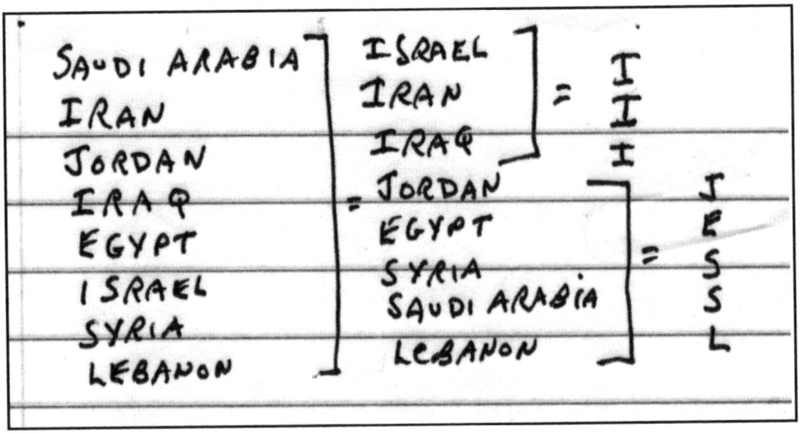

Illustration 3.4 Example of notes arranged in "chunks"

■ Summarize information with original language.

Summarizing calls on us to think carefully about the new information, digest it, and reduce it to its shortest version using the language of the original material. It is a powerful technique because it requires higher order thinking skills as when we reduce ideas to symbols. Auditory learners should summarize out loud before writing.

■ Paraphrase information with your words.

Paraphrasing is an even more powerful tool than summarizing for laying down strong, clear memory traces in semantic memory. Like summarizing, paraphrasing calls on higher order thinking skills, but this process cooks the ideas in the stew of your personal past experiences. When ideas are re-phrased in your own words, you have a sense of ownership of them and they are easier to recall. Semantic memory may be reinforced by connecting the new information to related emotional memories. Auditory learners should paraphrase out loud as well as writing them.

■ Write a test question.

Write the most thought provoking, hard questions about the new information by beginning with the words, how, why, and explain. Easier questions begin with the words, list, who, what, when, state, identify, define and describe. By phrasing questions you are reorganizing the data and digesting it. Writing questions helps cement the information in your semantic memory. Answering your own questions is even better! Both visual and aural learners will benefit from this technique.

■ Prepare a time line.

Timelines provide a strong, visual, symbolic representation of the events in historical sequence. By using scale to represent the passage of years, you help your brain absorb and hold difficult data. Include symbols above the dates in your timeline to further reinforce the events in your semantic memory. Kinesthetic and visual learners will benefit most from this technique, but aural learners should use it, too. See Illustration 3.5 on page 3-14 for an example of a student's timeline.

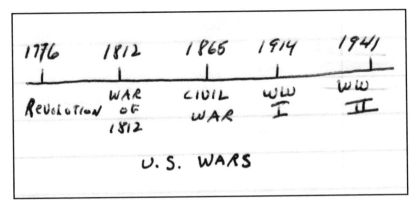

Illustration 3.5 Example of a timeline to represent historical events

■ Use mnemonics.

Write acronyms. Acronyms are groups of letters formed from the first letters of a group of words to make a new word. Our language is filled with acronyms. RADAR for Radio Detection and Ranging, NASA for National Aeronautics and Space Administration, and FAQ for Frequently Asked Questions are common acronyms.

You can invent your own acronyms for data you want to recall easily. Suppose you want to recall the major elements that make up our long term memory. They are Emotional, Automatic response, Procedural, Semantic, Episodic, and Spatial. Use the first letters of each word, EAPSES, and rearrange them so they form an acronym that is easy for you to remember. For example, SEPEAS might be good for you or SAPEES might be better.

Write initialisms. These are combinations of letters and numerals that usually cannot be pronounced as words. An example is CD for compact disc. Text messaging has created thousands of initialisms such as 2G2BT for too good to be true. Use your imagination to create initialisms to help strengthen your semantic memory.

Be aware that acronyms and initialisms only serve to jog memory. They do not help with comprehension. Moreover, not every data series will easily lend itself to the formation of acronyms or initialisms. Having too many to remember can cause more problems than you need, so limit them to the concepts that are most important.

Write acrostics. Acrostics are sentences formed from the first letters of words you want to remember. Acrostics have been used for centuries as tricks of language and as mnemonic devices. Instead of forming a single word as in acronyms, you create a whole sentence.

Remember this acrostic sentence for the musical scale? Every Good Boy Does Fine stands for the musical notes, EGBDF. Medical students have a host of acrostics to remember the physiology of the human body. Here is one for the bones of the skull. Old People From Texas Eat Spiders for Occipital, Parietal, Frontal, Temporal, Ethmoid, and Sphenoid.

If you want to remember several items, list them and try to make a sentence using the first letters of each item. You can make up an acrostic for the main ideas of an important lecture or the main parts of a book chapter. Mnemonics are great for visual and aural learners.

■ Use word and image association

Associate words with freaky images. Memory experts suggest associating new ideas that you want to remember with words or images that you know. Selecting silly or unusual links is a good technique.

Suppose you have trouble recalling the names of some of Abraham Lincoln's cabinet members. They were William Henry Seward, Secretary of State; Salmon P. Chase, Secretary of the Treasury; and Edward Bates, Attorney General.

Look at each name and link a word picture to it. These are easy. Here's how one student figured out a way to remember the names. Seward sounds like sewer. Salmon is a fish and there is a Chase there, too. Bates sounds like bait. He wrote the following sentence. "Edward used bait to chase salmon in William's sewer." You can use this technique in many situations. The quirkier your links, the more effective it will be. Aural and visual learners will do well using word and image association.

■ Recite in your own words.

Recitation is one of the most powerful of all the tools for getting data deeply into long term semantic memory! Because reciting involves the use of your vocal and hearing nerves and muscles, you will be adding layers of memory.

After you have thought about the information, recite it aloud in your own words. By using your own words you have taken ownership of the material. The information is no longer just notes in the words of your teacher or of the text writer. You have chewed, swallowed, and digested the data. It is now your own!

How often should you recite? Once is not enough! You must recite the information periodically in order to reinforce the clear, accurate, powerful memory traces. Every time you recite it is as if you are driving a car over the same tracks in a soft, grass field. The more often you do it, the deeper the tracks.

Reciting is difficult, but the more repetitions you make, the better you will be able to recall data when you need it to answer an examination question!

Recitation is a primary tool for auditory learners, but visual and kinesthetic learners must also use it. Kinesthetic types can walk around the room while reciting and visual learners may visualize or even scribble the words they are reciting.

■ Teach the material.

Teaching is one step above recitation. In order to teach you must have fully integrated the data or information into your long term memory.

You have absorbed and digested the information and reformulated it in your mind. By teaching the information you are once again recalling and reciting the data. When you teach, you must reconstruct the information.

If you have a group of friends who study with you, agree to have each of you teach the material. As you prepare your lesson you may find that you are not so sure about some areas. You will have to review those topics and improve your lesson plan.

Good teachers are prepared for questions from their students. Encourage your study mates to challenge you with questions. You may discover more areas that need beefing up.

Aural learners benefit from this procedure, but visual learners who prepare diagrams or charts for their lessons or who write on whiteboards or prepare handouts will also benefit.

BUILDING EMOTIONAL MEMORY

■ Relate the data to your personal life.

Get information into your emotional memory area. If you can do it, you will have two long term areas to draw upon. The emotional memory will reinforce the semantic memory.

The trick in studying is to try to find a way to relate what we have learned to our personal lives. Stock market traders can recall the stock symbols and prices of many companies. It is their intense motivation or emotional attachment that makes this possible. Most of us can remember more trivia about our hobbies than we can about school work because of our deep, personal interest. Try to develop a real interest in the subject you are learning and you will find yourself remembering more.

In the social studies area you may try to imagine yourself as a character. How would you have felt in Lincoln's shoes as he prepared the Gettysburg Address? You should try to become emotionally involved by imagining yourself debating an issue.

Try to think of other ways that the new material relates to your own life. How will this scientific discovery affect you and your offspring? How will it affect the way we live? If you believe the learning will be helpful to you or has some other emotional element, you will remember it more easily. Linking the new learning to some emotional event in your life is also helpful.

For example, if you are studying a play in English class, perhaps you can tie the learning to an experience you had acting in a school production. Learning about nativism and the Know Nothing Party in U.S. history may evoke an emotional reaction as you think of your feelings about the current immigration debates dealing with illegal aliens. Once done, you will access the new data through your emotional memory as well as your semantic memory.

BUILDING EPISODIC MEMORY

Episodic memory rarely needs beefing up. The events are usually so powerful that they remain in memory for quite a long time, especially because they are often linked with emotional experience. However, if an episode or event is related to something you are learning, it is worthwhile to take a few moments to reflect on the original episode and how it may impact on the new learning.

For example, if you have a strong memory of a very positive episode in a former history class when your teacher heavily praised your work, you might reinforce that memory and tie it to the history lecture in your current class.

Visualizing the prior event will help visual learners. Recalling the sounds and feelings of episodes will also be of value to kinesthetic and aural learners.

BUILDING AUTOMATIC RESPONSE MEMORY

Drill

Drills build automatic responses. Old fashioned drills are what built your automatic responses to multiplication tables. Use 3 x 5 inch cards. Write important information such as new vocabulary, dates, and events on one side and the answers on the other. Carry them with you and when you have a minute, take them out and drill yourself.

Aural learners will benefit from repeating the answers out loud while visual learners will find that visualizing the answers while repeating the words will be beneficial. Kinesthetic learners can get positive results by walking about while doing the drills.

Use Songs

Use a song melody to reinforce automatic responses. Do you remember how you first learned to recite the alphabet as a child? You sang it to the tune of "Twinkle Twinkle Little Star." Think of all the song lyrics you can sing in the shower. If you hear just the first few bars of music, you can probably sing all the words of the entire song. Songs and rhymes slip easily into long term memory and are very easy to recall. Think of all the songs, poems, and rhymes that you can recite almost at will.

Good aural and some visual learners can make up lyrics using the concepts they want to learn to fit a familiar tune. If you are good at writing musical parodies to old tunes, this may be an excellent way to get data into memory. Try using popular "raps" as a basis.

Perhaps you and some friends might make this part of a study session. Reciting the new rhyme or singing the new lyric a few times will make recall of the new data very easy. And it might be fun!

BUILDING SPATIAL MEMORY

Spatial memory, like episodic memory, has been built over time to give you clear knowledge of boundaries and the ability to navigate the environment. As you mature so does your spatial memory and your ability to understand relative distances and directions and to fully comprehend your relationship to your environment.

NOTE TAKING FIGHTS FORGETTING

This book is a prescription against forgetting. As you learn the skill sets of note taking, you will find that every one is based on the brain research about memory described in this chapter. Above all, make Bud's Note Taking System a regular part of your study habits.

Summary

This book is a prescription against forgetting. Brain scientists have provided us with a basis for understanding how we remember and learn.

You now know how procedural memory is the basis for note taking skills. You have learned several techniques to strengthen your semantic, emotional, episodic, automatic response, and spatial memories.

In Chapter 4, you will learn how to apply what you have learned to the procedural skill of note taking. You will see how note taking will implant strong, clear data in appropriate memories.

By using deliberate practice to master note taking from lectures, you will be able to more easily recall important information so you can ace your exams. Go to it!

Chapter 4
Take Great Notes In Class

You are now ready to begin training to be a champion note taker. Just as the olympic swimmer or skier trains, be prepared for some intensive work involving "deliberate practice." Remember, note taking is a skill that requires procedural memory training along the same lines as learning to play an instrument, to paint landscapes, to keyboard, or to play tennis or golf.

You must break the skill of note taking into its component parts, set a goal to master the first component, perform the component, evaluate how well you met your goal, adjust your technique to improve, and do it all over again many, many times. Practice, practice, practice.

Select A Training Site and Equipment

Concert pianists don't immediately go on stage in Carnegie Hall. They spend hours in rehearsal halls. Competitive sprinters don't just dash out to compete. They set up a training schedule of practice at a track. So you, too, will begin training for note taking before you use your skills in actual classes.

While you will not need the special track shoes, stop watch, athletic clothing or time at a practice track, you will need a few simple things to get started.

How do these sound?

Your Note Taking Training Equipment

Black or blue and red ball point pens.
A highlighter.
Your notebook with several pages prepared as shown on pages 4-4 and 4-5.

Your Note Taking Training Site
A quiet room.
Set up a small desk or table with a straight backed chair in front of a TV set to simulate a classroom setting.
Do not sit on a sofa or easy chair!

Training With TV Programs
Now you need someone to give a lecture so you can begin building your note taking skills! Guess what? Almost all day and night people are "lecturing" on TV! It is a perfect practice venue. Regular TV news presentations are usually short so they are great for your first trials. Later, as you gain confidence, check the TV listings to find longer, interesting C-Span, History, National Geographic and Discovery Channel programs. Look for public TV specials and political speeches. You might even choose some programs you have absolutely no interest in because that is a situation you will probably face in school.

Plan Your TV Training Schedule

Week 1: Plan a schedule of 3 daily spaced sessions of only 5 to 10 minutes !
Try for an early morning and evening session each day.
Week 2: Watch longer Discovery, C-Span or History, or Discovery Channel programs.
Complete all 8 tasks described in this chapter for every session.

Tape Recording
Tape recording, if allowed, is OK in a regular classroom. However, you should only use the recording to check on points you feel you may have missed. Listening to the full recorded lecture takes as long as the original and is a waste of time that you do not have. Note taking is NOT copying down everything the teacher or lecturer says!! Note taking is learning to listen for main ideas and supporting ideas and quickly writing them in your notebook.

HOW TO PREPARE YOUR NOTEBOOK

Academic note taking requires you to set up your notebook in a special way. This system was developed at Cornell University some years ago. While it may seem to take some time initially, you will find the preparation simple.

LEFT HAND PAGE

Top line: Course Name Topic Date

Second Heading: Future Assignment

Third Heading: Advance Organizer Questions

Fourth Heading: Maps, Diagrams, Charts, Timelines

Fifth Heading: Lecture Organization

Sixth Heading: Personal Statement

Seventh Heading: Possible Exam Question

RIGHT HAND AND FOLLOWING PAGES

Top line: Course Name Topic Date

Rule a vertical line two inches from the left edge

Label Right Column: Full Lecture Notes

Label Left Column: Personal Restatement

See the Sample Pages on 4-4 and 4-5.

Sample Left Hand Page

COURSE NAME   TOPIC   DATE
FUTURE ASSIGNMENT

ADVANCE ORGANIZER QUESTIONS

MAPS   DIAGRAMS   CHARTS   TIMELINES

LECTURE ORGANIZATION

PERSONAL STATEMENT

POSSIBLE EXAM QUESTIONS

THE LEFT HAND PAGE SHOULD LIKE THE ONE ABOVE

Sample Right Hand Page

Course Name	Topic	Date
Personal Restatents	Full Lecture Notes	

THE RIGHT HAND PAGE SHOULD LIKE THE ONE ABOVE

Should You Use Your Computer To Take Notes In Class?

OK, you're a tech junkie. You have an iPod, an iPhone, maybe even a new iPad, a Blackberry or other PDA, or a classy laptop. Microsoft's OneNote and WordPerfect's Lightning are proclaimed as terrific note taking software. There are even new tablet PCs that use a stylus to capture handwriting. So should you use your computer to take notes in class?

According to Nigel Ward, a computer professor at the University of Texas, "the short answer is probably not," although there are some advantages in computer note taking. Your notes could be more legible, more organized, and, as Ward says, you will impress your friends. The negatives are more work and computer demands that will make it hard to stay tuned to the lecture. OneNote and Lightning are designed for business users who have note taking needs that are markedly different from those of students. So for now, we'll say, "No!"

Components Of Note Taking Tasks

When we take a golf lesson, the pro carefully shows us all the components of the golf swing: the correct stance, the grip, the backswing, and follow through. Slowly, we try to get each of these components into our brains and bodies. We set our feet, check to see that our hands are properly placed on the club shaft, watch as we slowly start the backswing. And then comes the moment of truth. We are about to hit the ball. We swing hard and we --- miss the ball completely!

But this is how we learn new skills. At first we are not very successful, but by deliberate and motivated practice, we can make the skill occur spontaneously. Just as we can master golf, tennis, piano, and keyboarding, we can become star quality note takers!

This chapter breaks the entire process of note taking into eight major tasks. Each task involves several components. A golf game begins with a drive, followed by a fairway shot, then a pitch or chip and a final put. Each of these strokes has different components. We shift our stance, change the backswing, etc. So it is with note taking. Each note taking task has several components that you must learn just as you would learn the different parts of each golf stroke.

Task 1: Take Notes

> *WHAT BRAIN RESEARCH SAYS*
> If you are interested and motivated, new data will go to emotional and semantic memory. Strong visual and oral stimuli move into sensory memory and working memory where they connect with long term memory.

COMPONENT 1: Your own shorthand.

You need to shorten words, in order to write quickly to keep up with the TV commentator or your teacher. You can use well-known abbreviations and make up your own. Here are some examples.

1. Shorten words: info for information, def for definition, gov for government, etc.

2. Use symbols:

= for equals	+ for plus
> for greater than	< for less than
w/ for with	w/o for without
vs for against	sm for small
lg for large	s/b for should be
b/4 for before	i.e. for that is
vs for against	e.g. for for example
b/c for because	c.f. for compare
# for number	% for per cent

3. Omit short, unimportant words like a, the, and adjectives.

4. Use scientific symbols in math and science lectures.

5. Invent your own symbols and shorthand. For example, you can eliminate vowels in many words like this: glbl wrmg for global warming.

Suppose you heard during a History Channel program on the Treaty of Versaille that "The Ottoman Empire lost territory." You might write in your new shorthand what you see in Illustration 4.1. on the next page.

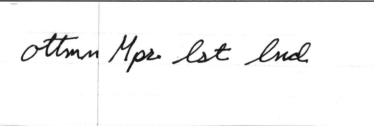

Illustration 4.1 Example of personal shorthand: Some vowels removed

COMPONENT 2: Advance Organizers

You must create an advance organizer about the TV program you are about to see by gathering information. Information gathering can be as simple as asking yourself what you already know about the subject, but it is better to do a quick Internet search. Based on your quick research, formulate questions you think the speaker will be able to answer. Jot them down on the top of the left hand page. By jogging your memory about the topic or doing a fast search, you stimulate your working memory as you get ready to receive more data. You are now prepped to get information. You are an active and participating note taker. You are prepared for the session! During regular classes you may get information from your teacher's outline, your text or even Google.

COMPONENT 3: Active Listening

You must train to be an active listener. Most students are apathetic when in class hoping for an entertaining lecture. You must sit erect. You must maintain eye contact with the TV commentator. You must concentrate. Your body language must show that you are interested. As the TV program proceeds, silently ask the speaker any of the questions you formulated. Don't react to the speaker's style, delivery or dress. Keep an open mind. Force yourself to be interested. A positive attitude is primary!

COMPONENT 4: Oral Cues

You must train to quickly identify oral cues. Speakers signal important ideas with word cues. You must develop an ear for word cues that will tell you significant information is coming. Here are a few oral cues: "important", "law", "theory", "effects", "summary", "main points", "outline", "causes", "conclusions", "remember this", "major point", "consequently." Pauses, repetition, changes in pitch, rate and volume of speech, **and** repetition of key words **let you know the** speaker is emphasizing important points. Be ready to copy data associated with these speech patterns. "For example" and "to illustrate" signal supporting data but not main ideas.

COMPONENT 5: Visual Cues

You must train to develop an eye for visual cues. Charts, graphs, bullet points, or outlines contain very important data. TV speakers emphasize important ideas this way. Be ready to focus on any visual cue.

Copy any diagrams, maps, or timelines at the top of the left hand page. Use an atlas later to clean up a map's accuracy. Illustration 4.2 below is an example of a map from a program on the history of Florida.

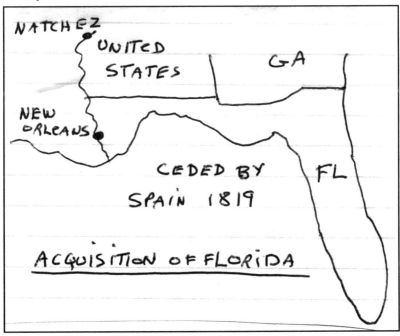

Illustration 4.2 Illustration of a map drawn on left hand page

COMPONENT 6: Speed Writing

This is a tough component that will require lots of deliberate practice. Write as legibly as you can in the Full Lecture Notes section of the right hand page. Speed is more important than legibility. You can always clarify scribbled and misspelled notes later. Don't try to write every word the TV commentator utters.

Listen. Then, using your "shorthand" quickly write the main points in simple outline form using phrases, words, or brief sentences. Separate main ideas from illustrations or examples.

Your First TV Practice Session

Check the TV listings to find a good program. CNN, CNBC, Fox, and MSNBC usually repeat brief news programs and interviews throughout the day. Locate an appropriate story, do a Google search, prepare an advance organizer and TAKE NOTES! Use deliberate practice!

Evaluate your practice sessions:

1. How effective was your advance organizer? Did it stimulate your interest in what the speaker had to say? Did you feel "smart" because you had advance information. Did you generate appropriate questions before the session?

2. How good was your shorthand? Did you use appropriate abbreviations and symbols? Did you memorize them all?

3. Evaluate your listening. Were you attentive and positive? Did you stay focussed? How was your body language? What could you do to improve your attitude?

4. How many oral cues did you pick up? What were they? Did they alert you to the most important ideas of the story? Did you find that the speaker used other cues? How many did you miss?

5. Were there any visual cues? What were they? Did you get any charts, graphs, or diagrams down on the top of the left hand page? Could you improve your speed in copying charts?

6. How fast were you able to write? Can you read what you wrote? Can you improve the percentage of main ideas you can get down with supporting illustrations and examples? Can you reconstruct the contents of the entire TV program from beginning to end from your notes?

Use deliberate practice of each component. Repeat your first trial with the same news story later in the day if possible. With each new TV program strive to improve in every component. Set targets for each.

Task 2: Read Your Notes

> **WHAT BRAIN RESEARCH SAYS**
> Working memory disappears quickly. Reading,
> identifying and digesting main ideas helps move data
> from working memory to long term semantic memory.
> Small "chunks" of data move more easily to semantic
> memory and are easier to recall.

Continue using deliberate practice. Keep working to improve each component.   Is your writing speed increasing?   Is your shorthand automatic? Do you get the oral and visual clues? Are you getting more main ideas down. Can you differentiate between main ideas and examples?

Practice, practice, practice! When you feel very competent in listening and writing, you are ready for Task 2: Read Your Notes. You now must get information from your short term and working memory into your long term memory banks

COMPONENT 1: Read Notes Hours After The TV Program

Read you TV practice notes a few hours after viewing to simulate the time lapse that normally occurs after a class lecture. Forgetting begins very quickly.

COMPONENT 2: Clean Up Illegible Scribbles and Clarify Items.

Scratch out any illegible words and rewrite them clearly.

Do not totally rewrite your notes. It simply takes too long and is not worth the effort. The idea in note taking is to to the job well enough the first time.

Clarify any items that are not clear. Check by reading your textbook or a Google source. In real classes you would make a note to ask your teacher about stuff you are not sure about. (Teachers like students who ask smart questions!).

COMPONENT 3: Underline or Highlight Main Ideas.

Check to be sure you have separated main ideas from illustrations or examples. Underline or highlight main ideas but not examples. See illustration 4.3 below for an example of underlining main ideas.

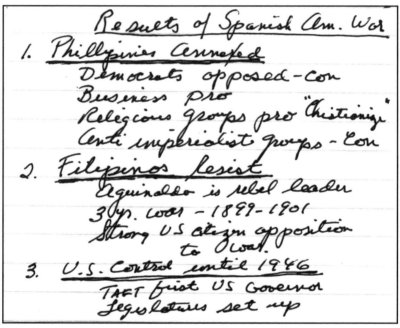

Illustration 4.3 Main ideas underlined but examples and illustrations not underlined.

COMPONENT 4: Move Main Ideas To Long Term Memory

Read the whole right hand page of your Full Lecture Notes. "Chunk" main ideas to make them easy to remember. See page 3-12. Without looking at your notes, try to recall the underlined or highlighted main ideas. Look back at your notes to see how successful you were in recalling the main ideas. Continue until you can recall all the main ideas without looking. You are putting strong, clear traces in long term memory.

Task 3: Restate the Main Ideas In Your Own Words

> *WHAT BRAIN RESEARCH SAYS*
> Semantic memory is enhanced when you absorb ideas, mentally digest them, and rephrase them. Symbols and pictures create an easy to remember picture in the brain that is associated with the original information.

ONLY COMPONENT: Rephrase Each Main Idea

Think of a single word or phrase that summarizes the first main idea. **Write that single word or phrase in the** Personal Restatement column on the left side of the right hand page.

Draw a representative symbol **next to the restatement if you can.** For example, in a lecture on the use of corn to make ethanol you **might have learned:** "Corn is good source for ethanol production." **You would re-phrase it as:**

"Corn = ethanol." **You might draw an ear of corn and a** gasoline can as shown in illustration 4.4 below.

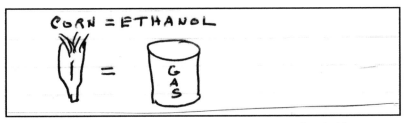

Illustration 4.4 Example of a symbol added to re-phrased main idea

Continue re-phrasing and drawing symbols **if appropriate for** each main idea.

Task 4: Recite Notes Based On Your Restatements

WHAT BRAIN RESEARCH SAYS
Reciting builds powerful semantic memory. Vocalizing brings the muscles and nerves of your vocal and auditory systems into play strengthening your long term semantic and conditioned response memory. Aural verbal learners love this, but visual learners must also use this procedure.

ONLY COMPONENT: Train Yourself To Recite

Cover the Full Lecture Notes on right side of the right hand page. Leave the Personal Restatement column exposed.

Look at the first Personal Restatement on the left side of the page. Recite aloud, in your own words, as much as you can of the first Full Lecture notes on the right side of the page.

Uncover your notes and check to see how much of the first Full Lecture notes you were able to recite.

Repeat as necessary until you can recite most of the Full Lecture notes of the first restatement.

Continue the process through each Personal Restatement on the left side of the right page of your notes.

Task 5: Identify the Lecture's Organizational Pattern.

> **WHAT BRAIN RESEARCH SAYS**
> Identifying the organizational pattern forces you to compare, associate, and analyze data. You "see" the structure and remember ideas better because they are part of a larger framework. Semantic memory is powerfully reinforced.

Now that you have finished the first four tasks, you are ready to review the entire lecture and decide what organizational pattern the lecturer used. By trying to identify the organizational pattern you are re-thinking all the data and seeing how it hangs together.

All lectures are (or at least should be) organized in some pattern. A lecturer discussing World War II might give a chronological view of the events or she might talk about the causes of the war. Another speaker might compare the results of WW I with those of WW II.

COMPONENT 1: Analyze All The Main Ideas

Answer questions like the following to help find the organizational pattern.

How did the lecture begin? How did it end?
Was the lecture a series of ideas in sequence?
Did it compare two or more ideas?
Did it show cause and effect?
Did the speaker present a problem and possible solutions?
Was a theory and the evidence to support it presented?

Select from the list below the organizational pattern of the lecture.

→ Sequential   → Trend

→ Chronological   → Cause & Effect

→ Categorical   → Comparison

→ Analytical   → Problem - Solutions

→ Theory - Evidence   → Event - Consequences

COMPONENT 2: Write A Summary Statement Naming The Organizational Pattern

Think through the answers to the questions on page 4-15. Think of the elements of the lecture to find its pattern. For example, a lecture describing an election and the activities that followed would be thought as an event and consequences organization. If the speaker discussed school bullying and described plans to stop it, you would identify it as a problem-solutions pattern. Your analysis of the lecture's organization will reinforce your semantic memory.

Write the statement in the Lecture Organization section on the left hand page of your notes as shown below in illustration 4.5.

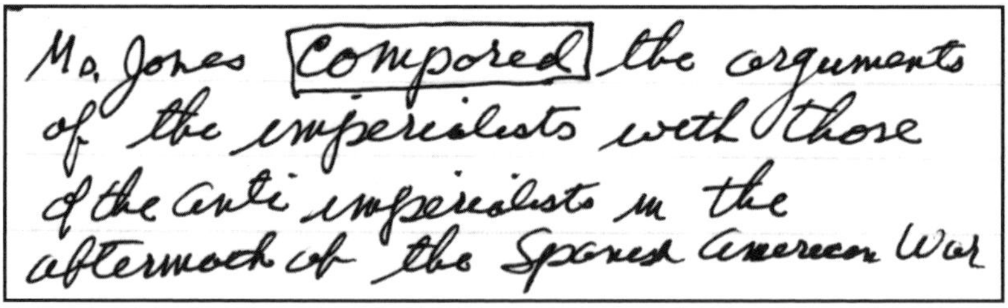

Illustration 4.5 Example of a comparison organizational pattern statement.

COMPONENT 3: Recite The Organizational Statement Aloud

Think about the way the lecture or program was structured as you recite aloud the statement you wrote describing the organizational pattern.

Task 6: Relate The Lecture To Your Own Life.

> ## WHAT BRAIN RESEARCH SAYS
> Hooking ideas to your personal views and values moves them to your emotional memory. You will have one of the most powerful long term memory areas to access when recalling information.

Even scientific data can evoke strong emotions. Studies of cancer research, for example can be related to personal experiences. Historical events, even those centuries old, can be related to your current belief systems. Literature can easily stoke a powerful, personal reaction.

COMPONENT 1: Ask Yourself Aloud A Series of Questions That Relate To Your Own Experiences.

Ask the following or similar questions.

What emotions do these ideas evoke in me? Do they make me angry, sad, upset?

Does the information remind me of any emotional event in my life? What was it? How are these ideas related to that event?

Have similar thoughts ever occurred to me? What are they?

Do I agree or disagree strongly? Why?

Do the ideas make me think of other questions?

Have I observed or experienced similar situations myself?

COMPONENT 2: Write Your Answers To These Questions Or Your Opinions And Reactions On The Left Page In The Personal Statement Section

> I was upset by the "White Man's Burden" attitude of Pres. McKinley toward the Filipinos. Carnegie said we civilized 8000 of them by sending them to heaven.
> I was surprised by the Chauvinistic feelings that many Americans had at the time.

Ilustration 4.6 Example of a statement that relates a topic to a student's personal belief system.

Rather than just remembering the facts of the Spanish American War, the student who wrote the Personal Statement above will remember how President McKinley's prosecution of the Spanish American War was very much at odds with his own feelings about human life. This association with the student's emotional memory will very strongly reinforce his semantic memory of the facts.

Tie new learnings to your own personal experiences to reinforce new learnings.

Task 7: Review and Recite Your Notes Frequently

> ### WHAT BRAIN RESEARCH SAYS
> Periodic reviewing and reciting are the most powerful techniques for building strong, clear memory traces in long term memory. Reviewing before new information is received ties the new to the older data already in memory.

After the first week of TV practice and you have completed Tasks 1-6 for each, take out the notes of the first program you watched. This is the hard part, making sure you have begun to move data from your short term memory to your long term memory banks.

COMPONENT 1: Each Week Review And Recite Tasks Four, Five, And Six

Reviewing prevents the forgetting process and reinforces long term memory. Spend about five or ten minutes on weekly reviews of each lecture.

Glance through your Personal Restatements of the first TV program on the left side of the right hand page   Look away. Try to recite as many of the main ideas as you can based on the restatements you wrote in Task 4.

Recite the statement of the Organizational Pattern of the lecture you wrote in Task 5.

Recite your Personal Statement relating to your personal feelings about the topic you wrote in Task 6 on the left hand page.

Keep at this task until you can recite all of the main ideas of the first program you watched. Repeat with all the other programs you watched.

COMPONENT 2: Before The Next Lecture Recite Tasks Four, Five, And Six of the Preceding Lecture.

You can't do this with your TV practice drills, but it is a must before each class lecture. Reciting before a new lecture will link the new material you are about to hear to the old information already in long term memory and make the new learning easier. This is the advance organizer step.

Recite your previous notes based on your Personal Restatements on the right hand page.

Recite the statement of the Organizational Pattern of the previous lecture.

Recite your comments and opinions about the topic that you wrote in the Personal Statement block on the left hand page.

COMPONENT 3: Use Mnemonics To Help To Help Memorize The Main Ideas of Your Training Sessions and Class Lectures.

Use acrostics, acronyms, word-image associations, and songs based on the data in your answers. Don't go overboard with this because overuse of mnemonics can cause confusion. See pages 3-14 and 3-15.

COMPONENT 4: Teach A "Lesson" On The Material Of Your First TV Program.

Teach a lesson to an imaginary class based on your first TV program. Use large cards instead of a blackboard for diagrams or notes. Start by stating what you are going to teach. Summarize after each main point. Include illustrations and examples. Be sure you have a final summary that covers all of the main ideas of your lecture. During regular classes actually teach a lesson to your study group.

Evaluate your teaching. Did you cover all of the main points. Did you "teach" with little reference to your written notes? Were you confident? Were you prepared to answer questions?

Task 8: Write An Exam Question Based On A TV Program

WHAT BRAIN RESEARCH SAYS
Writing questions forces you to use high level thinking skills. You must analyze and synthesize information to create good questions. Formulating questions strengthen long term semantic memory.

ONLY COMPONENT: Write An Examination Question In The "Possible Exam Question" Section On The Left Page Of Your Notes.

Think of the main ideas of the TV program. If you were the teacher, what questions would you want your students to be able to answer? In regular classes you would frame a question based on the last lecture.

Frame several questions preferably beginning with "why," "how," or "explain." Such questions require higher level thinking skills.

Frame other "fact" questions beginning with "list," "describe," "who," "what," "when," "where," "state," "define," or "identify." These require students to simply recall facts.

Now write the answers to the questions you framed. Look back at your notes to see how well you did. Did you ace the exam?

How did Pres. Teddy Roosevelt serve as a peace maker in the Russo - Japanese War?

Illustration 4.7 Example of one student's possible exam questions.

Taking Notes in Class
Typical Student's Handwritten Left Hand Page

Copy assignments here

Draw maps, diagrams, charts, etc. from board in top part of page.

Write organizational pattern statement here. This student decided lecture had a cause and effect organization as well as a categorical section. When recalling from long term memory, student will think of the effect and recall the causes: exploration, trade, and religion and the two categories of routes. This process strengthens long term memory.

Write how lecture relates to your personal experiences here. Note this student's response. This is a powerful way to reinforce long term memory.

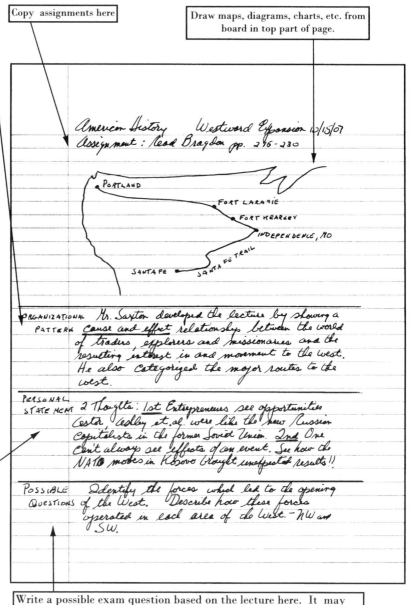

American History   Westward Expansion 10/15/07
Assignment: Read Bragdon pp. 216-230

PORTLAND
FORT LARAMIE
FORT KEARNEY
INDEPENDENCE, MO
SANTA FE   SANTA FE TRAIL

ORGANIZATIONAL PATTERN   Mr. Saxton developed the lecture by showing a cause and effect relationship between the world of traders, explorers and missionaries and the resulting interest in and movement to the west. He also categorized the major routes to the west.

PERSONAL STATEMENT   2 Thoughts: 1st Entrepreneurs see opportunities. Castor, Ashley et. al. were like the new Russian capitalists in the former Soviet Union. 2nd One can't always see effects of an event. See how the NATO moves in Kosovo brought unexpected results!!

POSSIBLE QUESTIONS   Identify the forces which led to the opening of the West. Describe how these forces operated in each area of the West. — NW and SW.

Write a possible exam question based on the lecture here. It may will be on the next test Note this student's question. Thinking of the question and answering it imbeds ideas in long term memory.

Taking Notes in Class
Typical Student's Handwritten Right Hand

This student started numbering main topics but didn't continue formal outlining. While doing Task 2, student added dashes, stars, and underlining for emphasis. Perfectly OK. Use the symbols and marks easiest for you.

Personal Restatement Column
Write summaries here.

Draw vertical line two inches from left edge.

Write full lecture notes here.

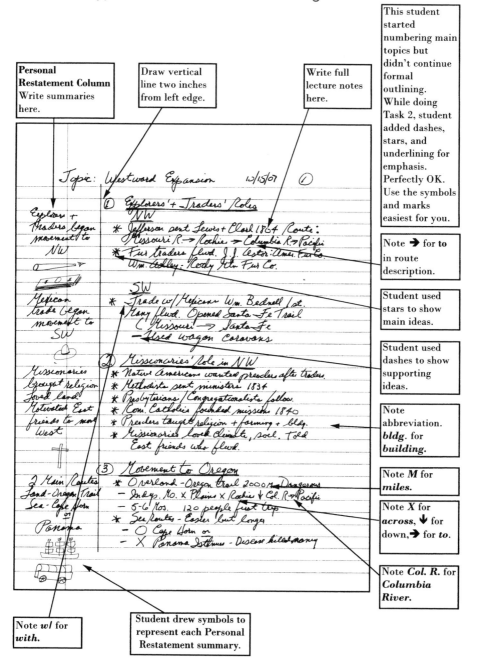

Note ➔ for **to** in route description.

Student used stars to show main ideas.

Student used dashes to show supporting ideas.

Note abbreviation. **bldg.** for **building**.

Note **M** for **miles**.

Note **X** for **across,** ⬇ for **down,** ➔ for **to.**

Note **Col. R.** for **Columbia River**.

Note **w/** for **with.**

Student drew symbols to represent each Personal Restatement summary.

4-23

PRACTICE, PRACTICE, PRACTICE

In order to develop a skill and embed it in your procedural memory you must practice, practice, practice until all the nerves and muscles are conditioned to respond automatically. You must use deliberative practice. See pages 3-6 and 3-7 for a review of this subject.

1. Perfect the memorization of your personal shorthand abbreviations. Decide on a target goal. For example, you want to write them all without error as a friend reads your list at a slow speed. Do it. Evaluate. Adjust. Repeat with a higher target speed and fewer misses.

2. Improve your speed writing. Decide on a target goal. For example, while watching short TV news programs you want to write legibly all the main points of the news in an organized outline form. Do it. Evaluate. Adjust. Repeat with a longer program. Keep at it until you can get down the main ideas, examples, and illustrations for a 30 minute TV special on the Discovery or History channels in acceptable handwriting.

3. Continue through all 8 tasks with deliberate practice until you are really proficient. When you are able to take notes "automatically" you will find your classes more enjoyable and you will meet with outstanding success in school.

The tough components of note taking are re-phrasing main ideas in your own words and reciting from memory. When you can recite your notes without peeking you have succeeded in mastering note taking in class and you are on your way to becoming an A+ student.

Note Taking Overload!!!

When you have mastered note taking in the practice TV sessions and start taking notes in regular classes you will find that you have many pages of notes to review and recite. It may seem that the load is impossible. How can you possibly keep all that information in semantic memory and recall it for exams? The answer is knowing what is really important and what is not. The answer is figuring out what your teacher will probably ask on exams.

There is a way and it's called the 80-20 rule!

Use The 80-20 Rule To Find What's Important

Back in 1902, an Italian economist, Vilfredo Pareto, noticed that 80% of the land in Italy was owned by 20% of the population. He also noticed that 80% of the peas in his garden came from 20% of the pea pods. Others have applied this finding to different circumstances. For example, businesses have noted that 80% of sales are derived from 20% of customers. Studies of the wealth of populations show that 20% of the people garner 80% of the income. Business managers know that 20% of work tasks take 80% of staff time and effort.

How can you apply this rule or principle to your work schedule. Analyze your daily and weekly schedule. Do you find that 20% of your tasks take 80% of your time? Those 20% are the ones that are most important and really significant. Those are tasks that are going to pay off. Therefore, if you have to leave some job undone, be sure it is not one of the 20%.

The Pareto Principle or 80-20 rule can be applied to your notes as well. Twenty percent of your notes are more significant and important than the remaining eighty percent. Not everything in your pages and pages of notes is of equal importance. The trick is to determine what is really important. Here are some suggestions:

> First, lecture introductions. Good teachers tell you what they are going to talk about. Get this stuff down.

> Second, anything written on a whiteboard or blackboard as a major concept, idea, rule, law, or definition.

> Third, charts, diagrams, and maps. They should be reproduced in your notes and the content reduced to writing.

> Fourth, summaries. Good teachers close with a summary of major points.

> Fifth, teacher handout material.

Budget your time wisely. Use the 80-20 rule to cut through the unimportant stuff and focus on the significant twenty per cent.

SUMMARY

You've learned to apply your knowledge of memory research to the skill of taking notes in class. If you have used deliberate practice to hone the components of all eight tasks, you are well on the way to becoming an A+ student. You are probably feeling better about yourself. You should be more confident when in class listening to your teacher and participating in discussions.

You are now an active learner. You are involved and ready to participate in class. You have developed a positive attitude toward school and you look forward to each class with anticipation because you are well prepared.

You are competently and confidently getting notes down quickly and clearly. You are identifying main ideas and supporting ideas and restating them in your own words.

You can identify the organizational pattern of a lecture and relate the lecture content to your own experiences.

You are reviewing and reciting your notes to reinforce all that you have learned. You can construct a tough exam question that you can answer.

By mastering the skill of taking notes in class, your grades on quizzes and tests should be good to great.

In Chapter 5, we turn our attention to the skill sets needed for taking notes from texts. Your mastery of note taking in class will be very helpful because some skill sets are similar. In one respect, taking notes from texts is easier because there is no need to absorb information and write quickly. But you will find the task just as challenging.

Chapter 5
Take Great Notes From Texts

When you read a textbook, you receive visual stimuli from the printed page. Immediately, as you read, connections are made to working memory and then to your long term memory banks. The new data tries to fit on any existing frameworks and connects with old data in long term memory. For example, if you are reading a new poem, information about the poem will hook on to already stored ideas of the poem's subject as well as rhyme, alliteration, and scansion. Emotional and episodic memories may also be stimulated by the new poem's content.

These connections help you to read, understand, digest, and get the new information into long term memory where it should be available for later use or when your knowledge will be tested on an examination.

As you know from the earlier chapters of this book, you must do everything you can to lay down powerful, clear ideas in your memory banks if you are to be successful in recalling and learning new information. In this respect, note taking from texts and note taking in class share the same goals.

SPECIAL SKILLS FOR TEXT NOTE TAKING

There are six tasks and associated components for text note taking. These differ somewhat from the tasks and components for class note taking. For example, there is no need for speed writing. Within limits you can work at your own rate and at your own time. Nevertheless, you will still need to use deliberate practice to hone your text note taking skills to get them embedded in your procedural memory and make them automatic.

Just as you learned to be an active listener, you will learn to be an active reader. By using your knowledge of brain research to take outstanding text notes you will approach your text reading with confidence. Instead of plodding through text pages with no idea of what is coming, you will be an active partner with the author. You will be way ahead of your more passive classmates.

Should You Use Your Computer To Take Notes From Texts Or Should You Handwrite?

The answer was "no" to using your computer when taking notes in class because for most students the difficulties outweighed the advantages. Foremost was the problem of keeping up with a lecturer while juggling mouse, keyboard and possibly a stylus. However, when taking notes from texts there is no speaker to follow and no rush to get notes down quickly. So the answer now is "yes" if you are comfortable with the hardware and software.

ADVANTAGES OF COMPUTER NOTE TAKING

First, your notes will be clearer and easier to read.

Second, it is simple to add enhancements such as changing type font and size, adding underlines, bolding, italics and even color to make words stand out.

Third, you can use the Insert Tab in Microsoft Word to add photos, tables, clip art, shapes, and charts. See page 5-8 for examples of what is possible.

Fourth, you can easily add information from your lecture notes to your class notes.

DISADVANTAGES OF COMPUTER NOTE TAKING

The handwritten method uses columns. Setting up columns in a handwritten notebook is simple. All you have to do is draw a vertical line down the page. Not so with computers. If you set up two columns on a Word page, you cannot jump from one column to the other. When you finish typing at the bottom of the the left column, your typing will move automatically to the top of the right column.

The decision to use the handwritten or computer method is yours. The skills are virtually the same. Read the instructions for both methods and decide which will be best for you. You can experiment and try both. Instructions for preparing notebooks for handwritten note taking are on pages 5-3 to 5-5. Instructions for preparing pages for the computer method are on pages 5-6 and 5-7.

Preparing the handwritten pages will help you understand the procedure for computer note taking. So even if you decide later to use the computer, prepare the handwritten pages.

HOW TO PREPARE YOUR NOTEBOOK FOR HANDWRITTEN NOTETAKING

LEFT HAND PAGE

See the next two pages for sample handwritten method pages.

1. Top line: Date   Text Title   Chapter   Pages

2. Draw a vertical line about six and a half inches down the center of the page.

3. Label top of left column: Outline

4. Label right column: Questions

5. Draw a horizontal line across the middle of the page

8. Rule three horizontal lines to divide the bottom of the page into four equal parts

9. Label Top Space: Chapter Summary

10. Label Second Space: Charts, Graphs, Maps, Pictures

11. Label Third Space: Possible Exam Questions

12. Label Fourth Space: New Vocabulary

RIGHT HAND AND FOLLOWING PAGES

1. Label top line: Date   Text Title   Chapter   Pages

2. Label top of page: Answers

Handwritten Method

Sample Left Hand Page

DATE	TEXT TITLE	CHAPTER	PAGES
OUTLINE		QUESTIONS	

CHAPTER SUMMARY

CHARTS   GRAPHS   MAPS   PICTURES

POSSIBLE EXAM QUESTIONS

NEW VOCABULARY

THE LEFT HAND PAGE SHOULD LOOK LIKE THE ONE ABOVE

Handwritten Method

Sample Right Hand Page

DATE	TEXT TITLE	CHAPTER	PAGES
	ANSWERS		

THE RIGHT HAND PAGE SHOULD LOOK LIKE THE ONE ABOVE

HOW TO PREPARE YOUR NOTEBOOK
FOR COMPUTER NOTETAKING

Although you can set up two columns in Microsoft Word by clicking on the Page Layout and Columns tabs, Word will not allow you to tab between the columns. Therefore, you must use two pages to replicate the handwritten right page. As a result, you will be working with three pages instead of two.

As you read these instructions, look at page 5-7.

1. Open a New Folder in My Documents. Label it with your course title such as History 103.

2. Open a new document in Microsoft Word. Save it as Master Page Outline. At the top of the page type these headings: Date, Title, Chapter, and Pages.
> On the next line center the heading: Outline.
> About half way down the left side of the page, type the heading: Chapter Summary.
> Skip three lines and type the heading: Charts, Graphs, Pictures.
> Skip three lines and type the heading: Possible Test Questions.
> Skip three lines and type the heading: New Vocabulary.

3. Open a second new document. Save it as Master Page Questions. At the top of the page type the same heading as you did for Master Page 1. Skip a line and center the heading: Questions.

4. Finally, open a third new document. Save it as Master Page Answers. At the top of the page type the same heading as you did for Master Page 1. Skip a line and center the heading: Answers.

5. When you are ready to begin reading in your text, open the three Master Pages, add the date, title, chapter and pages in the headings. If you were reading Chapter 13 in your text, you would save the Outline Page as: History Outline Ch 13, the Questions Page as History Questions Ch 13, and the Answers Page as History Answers Ch 13. Most likely your Answer document will extend to more than one page.

When you begin a chapter, just open the three Master pages and save them as shown above in 5. with the new chapter number.

Sample Layouts for Computer Note Taking From Texts

Master Page Outline

Date	Title		Chapter Pages
		Outline	

Chapter Summary

Charts, Graphs, Pictures

Possible Test Questions

New Vocabulary

Master Page Questions

Date	Title		Chapter Pages
		Questions	

Master Page Answers

Date	Title		Chapter Pages
		Answers	

If you click on the Insert Tab in Microsoft Word as shown below, you can enhance your notes with clip art, shapes, and charts.

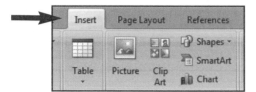

Just below are examples of what can be inserted.

Select Table: **You can Insert a table, draw your own table, or an Excel spreadsheet.**

City or Town	Point A	Point B	Point C	Point D	Point E
Point A	—				
Point B	87	—			
Point C	64	56	—		
Point D	37	32	91	—	
Point E	93	35	54	43	—

Select Insert Clip Art **A drop down list will appear where you can search for various subjects from your own photo files, Clip art, or from Clip online**

Select Shapes: **You can insert lines, basic shapes, block arrows, flow charts, and stars that can be embellished the shapes with color, colored outlines, and shadow.**

Select Smart Art: **You can insert various diagrams that portray cycles, relationships, and other forms that can be modified with varied layouts, colors, and styles.**

Select Charts: **You can insert column, line, pie, bar, area, and other chart types that can be modified with style and color. You can add your own text and data to the charts.**

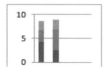

How To Train For Text Note Taking

In Chapter 1 you learned that we master skills through two basic steps. First, we identify each component of the skill. Second, we use deliberate practice to gradually master each component. In Chapter 4 you used this procedure to hone your class note taking skills.

To master note taking from texts you must follow the same methodology although there are only six tasks you have to learn. Some components are the same as those you used in taking class notes. Some are different.

Unfortunately, there can be no preliminary training exercises with a TV as you did learning to take notes in class. You more or less have to jump right into the deep end of the pool. Fortunately, you can take your time because you don't have to listen, keep up with a teacher or lecturer, or write fast in shorthand to get down the main ideas and other information.

Here is an overview (an advance organizer for you) of the skills involved in taking notes from a chapter in a text.

Task 1: You will get psyched and arrange your environment. You will select a room where there will be no distractions. You will gather all your study materials. You will be professional and positive.

Task 2: You will make an Advance Organizer by skimming the chapter you are about to read. You will prepare an Outline of the chapter.

Task 3: You will formulate Questions based on your Outline.

Task 4: You will read powerfully to find and write Answers to your Questions.

Task 5: You will recite each Answer and re-read the chapter quickly to check for accuracy.

Task 6: You will review your answers weekly. You will write test questions based on the information in the chapter.

The detailed components for each task follow.

Task 1: Get Psyched and Arrange Your Environment

COMPONENT 1: Establish A Positive Attitude

Approach the task positively. Sit at your desk or table on the edge of your seat. Be determined to get all you can from the text. Get rid of negative thoughts such as "This is too hard." or "How will I ever finish this assignment?"

Make a positive mental image of yourself working confidently through the text and succeeding. Repeat this "image making" twice a day for a minute or two every day you are taking notes from texts.

Relate the reading to your long term personal goals. Tell yourself, "When I master this reading, I will be on my way to an A." Remind yourself that you are an "active reader."

COMPONENT 2: Be Business-Like

Establish a business-like environment. Be sure you have a clean, well-lighted, study area without distractions of magazines, radio, or friends, although aural learners might benefit from some good background music. Use the library if your home base cannot provide a suitable environment. Be sure the lighting is good.

Have all materials at hand: The textbook, pens, hi-lighters, a good collegiate dictionary, your computer loaded with the appropriate Master Pages or your notebook if you are using the handwritten method.

Sit in a comfortable, straight backed chair at an uncluttered desk or table. Don't even think about reading on a sofa or in bed!!

Task 2: First Skimming Reading: Make an Advance Organizer

> **WHAT BRAIN RESEARCH SAYS**
> Semantic memory is enhanced when you add new facts to an organizational framework that already exists in you memory.

COMPONENT 1: Create an advance organizer.

An advance organizer provides the brain with a framework on which to attach new information.

Read the preface, introduction, or foreword if this is your first assignment in the text. In these sections you will find the author's motivation for writing the book.

Read the table of contents to get an overview of the scope of the text. You should see how each chapter contributes to the total work.

Read the printed summary at the beginning or end of the chapter if one is included. Summarize it in your own words under the heading Chapter Summary in your note pages.

Note page locations of charts, graphs, or pictures under the heading Charts, Graphs, Pictures.

Read end of chapter questions if they exist. Jot them down under the heading Possible Test Questions. Think of these questions as you read because the answers will be found in the text. Many teachers base test questions on those printed in texts.

Review your notes of the preceding chapter if this is not the first chapter in the text. Reviewing these notes will help you tie the information you are about to read in this chapter with the information you learned in the preceding one.

COMPONENT 2: Prepare an Outline

Skim through the chapter and read paragraph headings headings and sub-headings. Using the major headings and sub-headings of the chapter, make an outline on the "Outline" Page if computer note taking or the left column of the left page if handwriting.

The outline is a major part of your advance organizer. Use the Harvard outline or decimal form:

Decimal Outline
1. Main topic
    1. 1. Sub-Topic
    1. 2. Sub-Topic
        1. 2. 1. Sub-Topic
        1. 2. 2. Sub-Topic

Harvard Outline
I. Main topic
    A. Sub-topic
    B. Sub-topic
        1. Sub-topic
        2. Sub-topic

You now have the big picture before you begin reading. You know what the writer is going to discuss. You have questions that the chapter will answer. You are an active reader!

COMPONENT 3: Identify The Organizational Pattern Of The Chapter

Examine the outline to determine how the author has arranged the information in the chapter.

Answer questions like the following to find the organizational pattern:

How did the chapter begin? How did it end?
Did the chapter describe a series of ideas in a sequence?
Were two or more ideas compared?
Did the author show the effect(s) of a cause?
Did the author present a problem and possible solutions?
Was a theory and the evidence to support it presented?

Select from the list below the name of the organizational pattern of the chapter.

→ Sequential → Trend

→ Chronological → Cause & Effect

→ Categorical → Comparison

→ Analytical → Problem - Solutions

→ Theory - Evidence → Event - Consequences

COMPONENT 4: Learn New Vocabulary

Skim the chapter for special technical vocabulary. It is vital that you understand the unique vocabulary of each subject. Reading without first mastering these terms will severely limit your ability to understand and learn the material.

Look for a glossary at the end of the chapter. If there is one, copy definitions on 3 x 5 inch cards. Many texts print special words in bold and/or italics the first time they are used. Memorize the definitions.

Find unfamiliar vocabulary words by skimming the chapter. Copy each new vocabulary word on a 3 x 5 inch card and look up its meaning in a good, collegiate dictionary or in Internet dictionaries. Write the definition, etymology, and a piece of the sentence in which you found the word to learn it in the context in which it was used.

Write the special technical vocabulary and unfamiliar vocabulary words under the heading "New Vocabulary" on the Outline Page if computer note taking or the left page if handwriting.

Find new vocabulary words in your daily reading of newspapers and magazines. Add any other new words to your pack of cards. Carry the cards with you and recite the meanings whenever you get a minute. The richer your vocabulary, the more your comprehension and reading speed will improve.

By reading chapter summaries, reading end of chapter questions in the text, outlining, analyzing the chapter organization, and learning new vocabulary you are anticipating what the author is going to impart. You are not waiting to wade into the first paragraph with no idea of what you are about to learn. Passive readers do not take the steps you have taken. You are an active reader!!

Task 3: Formulate Questions

> ***WHAT BRAIN RESEARCH SAYS***
> When a criterion task, or what you need to learn, is clear you learn more easily. By preparing questions you set the criterion task and you focus clearly on what you have to learn.

ONLY COMPONENT: Formulate Questions Based On Your Outline.

Re-phrase as questions the headings you wrote on the "Outline" column and write them under the heading, Questions, on the Questions page if computer note taking or the right column of the left page if handwriting.

For example, the topic in the Outline shown on page 5-22: Election of 1848, becomes the question:

"What was the major issue of the election of 1848?" shown on page 5-23.

The sub-topic in the Outline shown on page 5-22: Democrats and Whigs becomes the question:

"What were the positions of the Democrats and Whigs?

You might add other questions that come to mind in addition to those suggested by the outline topics. Use the 5 w's (Who, What, Why, Where, When) and How to plan questions. The "how" and "why" questions are best. If the author has printed end of chapter questions, you might include some of them as well.

You are establishing a "criterion task" that tells you what you must learn. You are way ahead of passive readers who have no idea of what the author is going to discuss. You are an active reader!!

Task 4: Intensive Reading: Find Answers To Your Questions

> **WHAT BRAIN RESEARCH SAYS**
> You will remember more if you are motivated to learn, if you link new facts to the advance organizer, and if you make the learning meaningful. It is easier to learn if you break material into small chunks.

COMPONENT 1: Stay Focused And Motivated

Prepare psychologically. Understand that textbook reading is difficult. Psych yourself as if you were about to climb a mountain or attack some other physical task. Make a mental image of yourself succeeding.

Stay motivated. Don't approach the reading in anger toward your instructor because you think he or she was mean to assign this difficult material. Think about the value you will get from the reading, about how it will help raise your grade, and about how it will affect your career. You are doing this for you. Stop for a minute and again make a mental image of yourself succeeding with this assignment.

COMPONENT 2: Read Actively

Read carefully the opening and closing paragraph sentences. Most writers hand you a topic sentence at the beginning of each paragraph to let you know what will follow and end with a summary sentence or two.

Look for word cues such as bold headings and italics. Main ideas are often introduced by words like *"In conclusion," "to summarize," "consequently,"* and *"therefore."* Transition words such as *"furthermore," "moreover,"* signal important data coming. The words, *"but," "otherwise," "although" "on the other hand,"* forecast opposing ideas. Order words such as *"first," "second,"* and *"finally,"* highlight a series of significant points. *"For example,"* or *"to illustrate"* let you know what follows is not a main point.

Write definitions of difficult vocabulary in the margins near the words in the text to help with understanding.

Do not highlight yet. Before you know it, you will be highlighting too much. Make check marks or notes in the margin if you own the book. These can be erased or left when you have a better idea of what is important.

Recite aloud in your own words what you have read at the end of each paragraph as you go along.

Read critically. Is the author stating facts or opinions? Is the author biased? Do you agree with the author's conclusions? How does this author's ideas fit with the ideas of others? How does the text relate to the lecture notes you took in class?

Problem understanding? Put a big question mark in the margin and make a note to ask your teacher to explain in class. Continue reading. The following material may help you understand the passage that troubled you.

COMPONENT 3: Break The Reading Into Smaller Chunks

Plan to read "chunks." Remember the Magic 7. Don't try to read difficult material in a single, long session.

Read for 30 minutes and take 5. Get up and walk about. Have a cup of coffee or a glass of milk. You cannot easily transfer large quantities of material into long term memory in one sitting.

COMPONENT 4: Find The Answers To Your Questions

Read strategically. As you read each paragraph or page, be sure you are reading to get the answer to one of your listed questions.

Write the "Answers" to your "Questions" on the Answer page if computer note taking or the right page if handwriting. Use your "shorthand."

Insert diagrams, maps, symbols, graphs, and timelines anywhere on the "Answer" page to reinforce semantic memory. Study all charts, diagrams, symbols, timelines and graphs in the text and summarize what they describe.

Relate the information to your personal life. Does the reading remind you of an emotional event in your life? Do the ideas affect you emotionally? Do you agree or disagree strongly? Do these ideas upset you? Do they make you angry, sad, or happy?

COMPONENT 5: Strive To Increase Reading Speed

Read rapidly, but not a a speed that interferes with comprehension. Move a 5 x 8 inch card down the page above the line you are reading to prevent eye regressions or looking back at words you have already read.

Reduce the number of eye fixations on each line. Try not to read one word at a time, but rather strive to "take in" whole phrases or groups of words in each fixation.

Set a time limit. Don't drag on endlessly. Set a good pace and keep at it.

Read easy material at the rate of fifteen to twenty pages per hour. Difficult stuff will take much longer.

Don't attempt to match the ridiculous "speed reading" claims of being able to read a whole page in one glance suggested by some "speed reading" gurus. In general, comprehension improves with increases in speed and speed increases with improvement in comprehension. Good average speed is 250 words per minute.

Task 5: Recite

ONLY COMPONENT: Recite

Look at the first question you asked on the Question page if computer note taking or the right column of the left page if handwriting.

Quickly, read the first section of the text again. Check the answer to the first question you wrote in your notebook. Is it accurate? If not, revise it.

Recite the answer to the first question out loud without looking at your notes. Check to see if you recited correctly. Recite the answers to all your questions.

Recite as much of the chapter summary in the text and/or the one you wrote in Task 2. Check for accuracy.

Stress the recall of major concepts rather than details.

Do one more quick reading of the text with your highlighter. Now that you know which parts of the text are truly important, you can highlight your handwritten notes or add color or other enhancements to your computer notes as described on page 5-8. The highlighted words and phrases will help you during reviews. If you own the text, highlight only the important sentences.

Use mnemonics: acronyms, acrostics, word-image associations and songs to bolster your memory. Write them somewhere on the Answer page(s).

Think about any emotional link you may have to the topic. Have you had a similar experience? Can you tie the information you are reading to some emotional event? Try to get your emotional memory tied to the semantic memory you are building. Make a note on the Answer page(s) of your reactions.

Task 6: Review

WHAT BRAIN RESEARCH SAYS
Periodic reviews reinforce semantic and other long term memory banks by carving deep, clear memory traces. Each review strengthens the memory.

COMPONENT 1: Review Frequently

Recite the answers to your questions the day after your first reciting session. You may have forgotten some information, but it will quickly come back.

Each week spend five minutes to review your notes. Recite the main ideas and answers to questions.

Before tests, review your notes. Recite the main ideas, and answers to your questions for all the units that will be tested.

COMPONENT 2: Write A Test Question

Use "how," "why, and "explain" to open questions that will elicit in-depth responses.

Use 'who," "what", "when," "list," "define," and "describe" to elicit factual information. Write the answers to your questions.

Add your questions in the Possible Exam Question section on the Outline page for computer note taking or the left page for handwritten note taking.

COMPONENT 3: Teach A Lesson

Teach a lesson based on the chapter to an imaginary class or to a group of friends with whom you study. Use the answers to your questions as a basis for the lesson. Begin by telling the group what they will learn. Give them the main points of the chapter. Plan some challenging questions for your "class." Summarize the main points of the chapter at the end of the lesson.

Taking Notes From Texts
Typical Student's Handwritten Left Hand Page

Task 2. Begin developing an advance organizer by quickly copying major heads and sub-heads of the chapter using Harvard outline style in the left hand column.

Task 3. Rephrase the headings as questions in the right hand column.

Task 2. Continue development of the advance organizer by summarizing printed chapter summary.

Task 2. Describe illustrations, charts, diagrams, etc. This sample describes a brochure, *Emigrants Guide to California* which appears in this text.

Task 3. Write additional questions based on an overview printed at the beginning of the chapter.

Task 2. Write new, special vocabulary words This student found *popular sovereignty.*

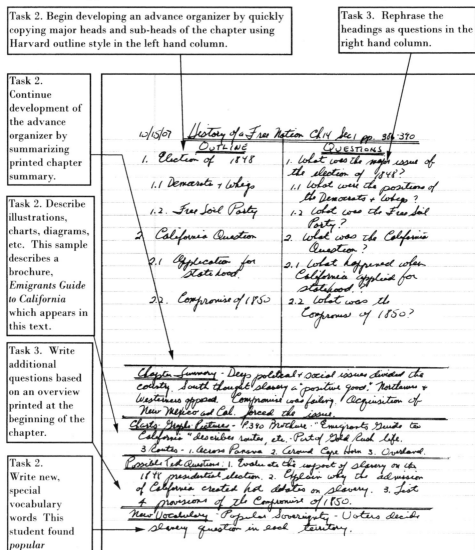

10/15/07 History of a Free Nation Ch 14 Sec 1 pp. 386-390

OUTLINE	QUESTIONS
1. Election of 1848	1. What was the major issue of the election of 1848?
1.1 Democrats + Whigs	1.1 What were the positions of the Democrats + Whigs?
1.2 Free Soil Party	1.2 What was the Free Soil Party?
2. California Question	2. What was the California Question?
2.1 Application for Statehood	2.1 What happened when California applied for statehood?
2.2 Compromise of 1850	2.2 What was the Compromise of 1850?

Chapter Summary - Deep political + social issues divided the country. South thought slavery a "positive good." Northerners + Westerners opposed. Compromise was failing. Acquisition of New Mexico and Cal. forced the issue.

Charts - Graphs - Pictures - P.390 Brochure. "Emigrants Guide to California" describes routes, etc. Part of Gold Rush life. 3 Routes - 1. Across Panama 2. Around Cape Horn 3. Overland.

Possible Test Questions: 1. Evaluate the impact of slavery on the 1848 presidential election. 2. Explain why the admission of California created hot debates on slavery. 3. List 4 provisions of the Compromise of 1850.

New Vocabulary - Popular Sovereignty - Voters decide slavery question in each territory.

The headings, sub-headings, description of the illustration, and other information on these pages were drawn from:

Bragdon, Henry W., Samuel P. McCutchen, and Donald A. Ritchie. *History of a Free Nation.* New York: Glencoe/McGraw-Hill, 1998. Chapter 14, Section 1.

5-20

Taking Notes From Texts
Typical Student's Handwritten Right Hand Page

Task 4. Read powerfully to find the answers to the questions based on the headings and sub-headings. Write answers on the right hand and following pages.

Read difficult passages aloud.

Stop at the end of each paragraph and explain aloud what you read.

Write answers to each question after reciting aloud.

Try to increase speed and comprehension.

10/15/07 History of a Free Nation Ch. 14 Sec 1 pp. 386-390

ANSWERS

Election of (1.) Issue - How to deal with slavery in newly
1848 acquired territories of Colorado and New Mexico.
1.1 _Democrats_ controlled by Southerner nominated
Democrats, a Northerner, Lewis Cass, supporter of popular sovereignty
Whigs ; Whigs, mostly Northerners, nominated Zachary
Taylor, Southern slave holder!! Whigs avoided
slavery question - stressed Taylor's military deeds.
Free 1.2 _Free Soilers_ - Emerged as 3rd Party from anti-
Soilers slavery North Democrats & "Conscience Whigs." - Motto:
"Free Soil, Free Speech, Free Labor, Free Men" Nominated
Van Buren. Deprived Cass of N.Y.'s 36 Electoral Votes!!

California (2) After gold discovered 1848, population grew by 95,000
Question and the slavery question arose.
2.1 _Statehood_ - Military could not stop crime-violence
Application Taylor called convention 1849 to set up gov't & forbid
slavery. Applied as free state, giving free states majority
South threatened to secede.
2.2 _Compromise_ - Henry Clay arranged.
Compromise Noted - 1. Cal. admitted as Free State
of 1850 2. Slave trade, not slavery forbidden in
D.C.
South 1. Stronger fugitive slave law passed
2. Mexican Cession - Divided Utah &
New Mexico into 2 territories with slavery
question decided by popular sovereignty
Compromise proved to be only
a temporary truce.

Task 5. Read first section of text again and check written answer for accuracy. Look away from notes and recite answer to first question.

Task 5. Read printed chapter summary again and recite your written summary on left page.

Task 5. One last reading to highlight important words.

Task 6. The day after the third reading in Task 5 recite the answers to the questions on the left page without looking at your notes. Spend just 10 minutes reciting. Once weekly spend 5 minutes reciting the answers. Before tests, recite the answers again.

Taking Notes From Texts
Typical Student's Computer Outline Page

May 4, 2010	**History of a Free Nation**	**Chapter: 14**	**Pages: 386-390**

Outline

1. Election of 1848

    1.1. Democrats and Whigs

    1.2. Free Soil Party

2. California Question

    2.1. Application for statehood

    2.2. Compromise of 1850

Chapter Summary

Deep political and social issues divided the country. South thought slavery a "positive good." Northerners and westerners opposed. Acquisition of New Mexico and California forced the issue.

Charts, Maps, Pictures

Page 390: See the picture of the brochure titled: Emigrants Guide to California" describing routes, etc. Part of the Gold Rush life. Three routes:1. Across Panama. 2. Around Cape Horn. 3. Overland

Possible Exam Questions

1. Why was slavery an important issue in the 1848 election?

2. Why was the Free Soil Party formed?

3. List four provisions of the Compromise of 1850.

New Vocabulary

Popular sovereignty - Voters decide slavery question in each territory.

Notes From Texts
Typical Student's Computer Questions Page

May 4, 2010   History of a Free Nation   Chapter: 14   Pages: 386-390

Questions

Questions from Outline

1. What was the major issue of the election of 1848?

    1.1. What were the positions of the Democrats & Whigs?

    1.2. What was the Free Soil Party?

2. What was the California Question?

    2.1. What happened when California applied for statehood?

    2.2. What was the Compromise of 1850?

Possible Exam Questions

1. Why was slavery an important issue in the 1848 election?

2. Why was the Free Soil Party formed?

3. List four provisions of the Compromise of 1850.

On page 5-22, a typical student's Outline on the Outline page is shown. The student created his advance organizer as described in Task 2. He wrote the Outline based on the major headings he found in the text. He read the summary in the text and summarized it in his notes. He posted questions he found at the end of the chapter under the Possible Exam Question heading. He used red to highlight main topics, black for sub-topics. He embellished his notes with a clip art of a ballot box and a map of California. Then he added a colored arrow to highlight what he thought was an important question.

On the Question page shown on this page, the student formulated questions based on the Outline. He has the "big picture" of the chapter and is psyched to find detailed answers. He is an active reader rather than one who has no idea what is coming and who does not have the advantage of an advance organizer!

Taking Notes From Texts
Typical Student's Computer Answer Page(s)

| May 4, 2010 | History of a Free Nation | Chapter: 14 | Pages: 386-390 |

Answers

1. Major Issue of Election of 1848: How to deal with slavery

in newly acquired territories of Colorado and New Mexico

       1.1 Democrats controlled by southerners, nominated Lewis Cass, a supporter of popular sovereignty. Whigs, mostly northerners, nominated Zachary Taylor, a southern slave holder!! **Whigs avoided the slavery question - stressed Taylor's military deeds.**

       1.2. Free Soilers - Emerged as 3rd party from anti-slavery northern Democrats and "Conscience Whigs" **Their motto:"Free Soil, Free Speech, Free Labor, Free Men" They nominated Van Buren and deprived Cass NY State's 36 electoral votes.**

       2. Major Issue California Question: after gold was discovered in 1848, population of California grew by 95,000 and the slavery question arose.

       2.1. Statehood question. Military could not stop crime and violence. Taylor called a convention in 1847 to set up a government and to forbid slavery. California applied as a free state giving the Free states a majority. The South threatened to secede.

       2.2. Compromise: of 1850. by Henry Clay.

North: California admitted as a Free State – Slave trade forbidden in South:
South: Stronger fugitive slave law passed.

On the Answer page shown on page 5-24 the student wrote the answers to the questions he formulated in Task 3. Note that he selected red font color to highlight the two major issues with blue and purple for the sub-issues. He inserted a clip art illustration of slave owners directing slaves, a picture of Zachary Taylor, and a picture of miners panning for gold in California. He also used colored arrows to point out important issues. Planning and inserting the embellishments will help to reinforce the information in your semantic memory.

Your Outline, Question, and Answer pages are not restricted to one page. You can add as many pages as necessary to each document.

Summary

If you are motivated to become an A+ student and if you have made note taking an automatic skill by applying the techniques outlined in this book, you have seen your grades improve. No doubt, too, your teachers have noted your outstanding class and test performance.

The skills you have learned will be helpful in many of your future school, professional, or business activities. The ability to "keep up" with discussions in different situations, take clear notes, and, above all, to get the data into your long term memory for future recall will bear great dividends.

You will be able to read texts, journal articles, and professional or business reports rapidly and with understanding! As you go through life, you will be amazed at the amount of information in print, on the Web, or in meetings that you are required to absorb and recall. Your newly learned automated note taking skills are powerful tools that will give you many advantages.

Good luck with your new skills in school and life!

Bibliography

Goleman, D. *Emotional Intelligence*. New York: Bantam, 1995.

Hudman, Andy. *Learning and Memory*. New York, NY: Chelsea ` House, 2006.

Jensen, Eric. *Teaching With the Brain In Mind*. Alexandria, VA: Association for Supervision and Curriculum Development, 1998.

Jensen, Eric. *Enriching the Brain*. San Francisco, CA: Jossey-Bass, 2006.

Kandel, Eric R. *In Search of Memory*. New York, NY: W. W. Norton, 2006.

Kensinger, E. A. and S. Corwin. "Memory Enhancement for Emotional Words." *Memory and Cognition* 31 (2003): 1169-1180.

Klingberg, Torkel. *The Overflowing Brain*. New York, NY: Oxford University Press, 2009.

Miller, George A. "The Magical Number Seven, Plus or Minus Two: Some Limits on Our Capacity for Processing Information." *The Psychology Review* 63 (1956): 81-97.

Sousa, D. *How Your Brain Learns*. Reston, VA: NAASP, 1995.

Sprenger, M. *Learning and Memory*. Alexandria, VA: Association for Supervision and Curriculum Development, 1999.

Tulving, E. "Episodic Memory From Mind To Brain." *Annual Review of Psychology* 53 (2002): 1-25.

Notes:

Notes: